THE ⬛ TIMES

MindGames
Word Puzzles
& Conundrums

Book
3

Published by Times Books

An imprint of HarperCollins Publishers
Westerhill Road
Bishopbriggs
Glasgow G64 2QT
www.harpercollins.co.uk
timesbooks@harpercollins.co.uk

First edition 2018

ISBN 978-0-00-828534-0

10 9 8 7 6 5 4 3 2

If you would like to comment on any aspect of this book, please contact us at the given address or online.
E-mail: puzzles@harpercollins.co.uk

facebook.com/collinsdictionary　　　@collinsdict

Printed and bound in Great Britain by CPI Group (UK) Ltd, Croydon, CR0 4YY

Acknowledgements

Codeword	PUZZLER MEDIA
Lexica	VEXUS PUZZLE DESIGN / LAURENCE MAY
Polygon	ROGER PHILLIPS
Quintagram® Concise	DAVID PARFITT
Quintagram® Cryptic	ed. RICHARD ROGAN
Wordwatch	JOSEPHINE BALMER and PAUL DUNN

Quintagram® is a registered trade mark of Times Newspapers Limited

MIX
Paper from
responsible sources
FSC™ C007454

This book is produced from independently certified
FSC™ paper to ensure responsible forest management.

For more information visit: www.harpercollins.co.uk/green

Contents

Introduction

Newspapers are built of words. Often these words are used to convey grave news, challenging opinion and sagacious insights. But they are also used for lighter purposes — and nowhere more delightfully than in the MindGames section of *The Times*.

We have reached Book 3 in our *Mind Games: Word Puzzles & Conundrums* series, and it's time for the latest puzzle innovation from *The Times* to make its debut. As well as featuring the fantastic foursome of Polygon, Lexica, Word Watch and Codeword, this edition introduces Quintagram®, a brand-new take on the traditional crossword. Each Quintagram® consists of five crossword-style clues to be solved in the usual way. The twist is that there is no grid. Instead, all the letters from the answers are provided in alphabetical order under the clues. When you work out an answer, cross off the corresponding letters, and this will whittle down the letters available for the remaining clues. There are two flavours of Quintagram®: Concise and Cryptic — and here we print 64 of each type. You'll be grateful we haven't stinted on quantity because once you've done one Quintagram®, I can guarantee you'll be dying to get started on the next!

David Parfitt
Puzzles Editor of *The Times*

For more MindGames, subscribe to *The Times* at:
store.thetimes.co.uk

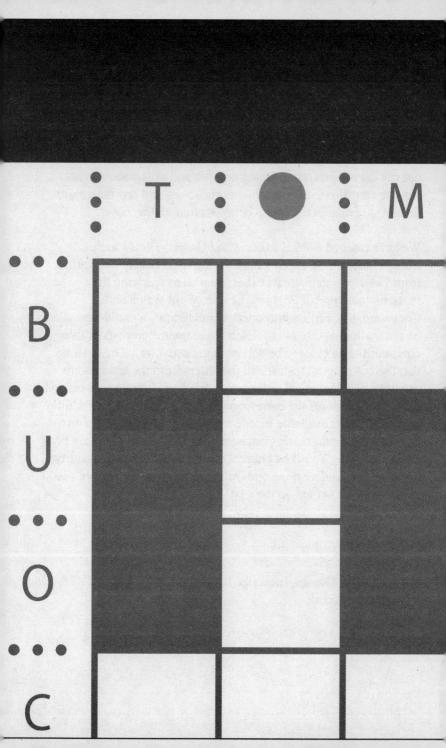

Lexica

T O Y

L

T

R

How to Play

Slide the letters around the outside back into the grid either horizontally or vertically.
Letters can slide over each other but must stay in their original row or column.

9

1

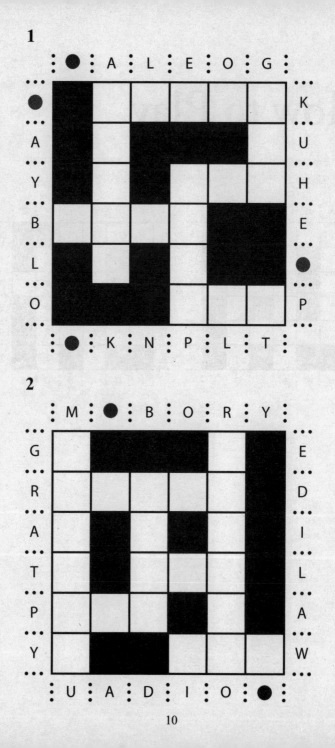

2

3

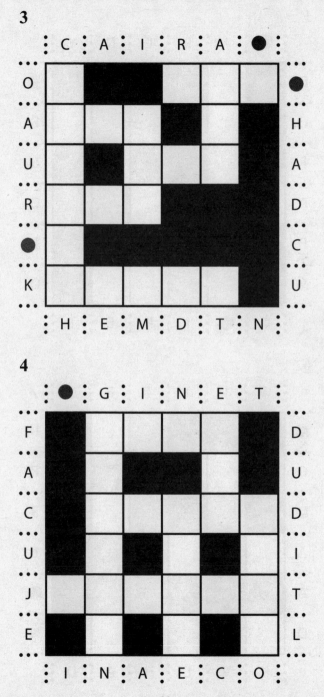

Top: C A I R A ●

Left: O A U R ● K

Right: ● H A D C U

Bottom: H E M D T N

4

Top: ● G I N E T

Left: F A C U J E

Right: D U D I T L

Bottom: I N A E C O

11

5

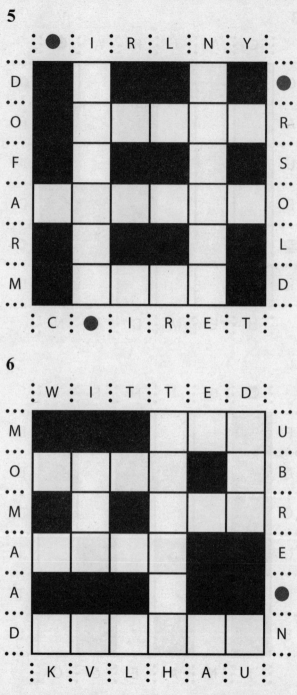

6

7

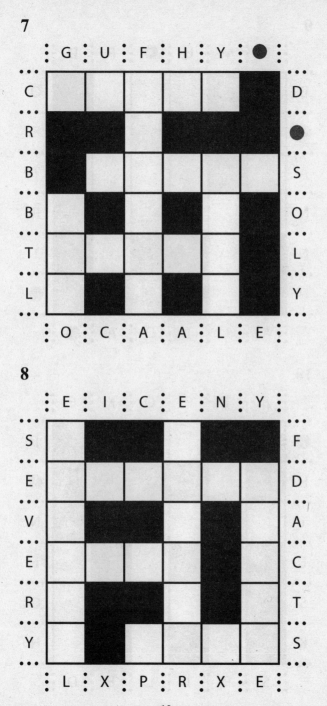

8

9

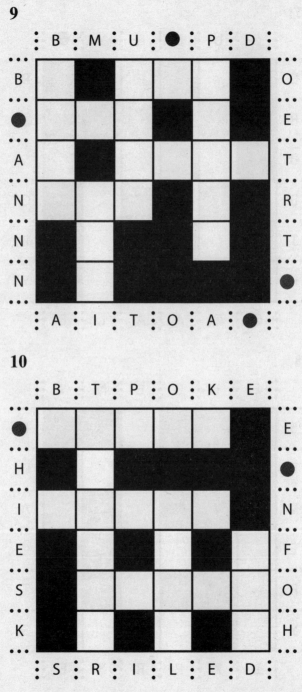

10

11

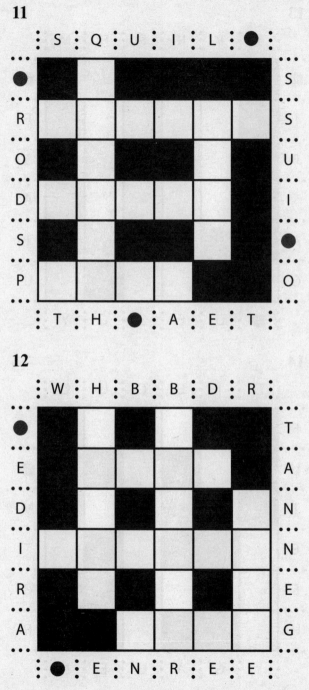

12

15

13

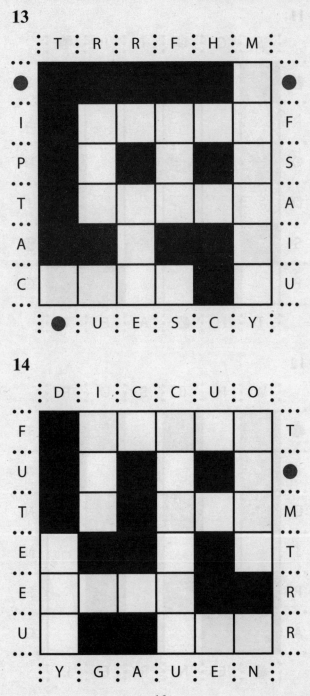

14

15

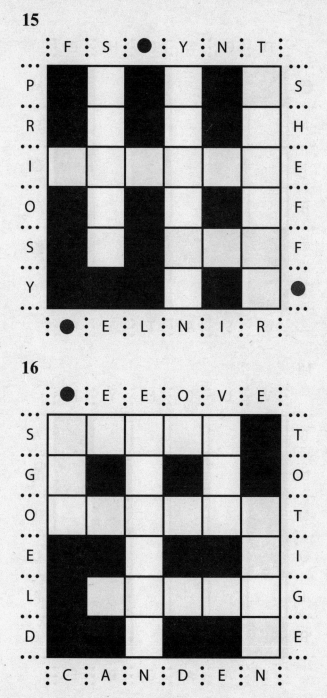

16

Top (15): F S ● Y N T
Left (15): P R I O S Y
Right (15): S H E F F ●
Bottom (15): ● E L N I R

Top (16): ● E E O V E
Left (16): S G O E L D
Right (16): T O T I G E
Bottom (16): C A N D E N

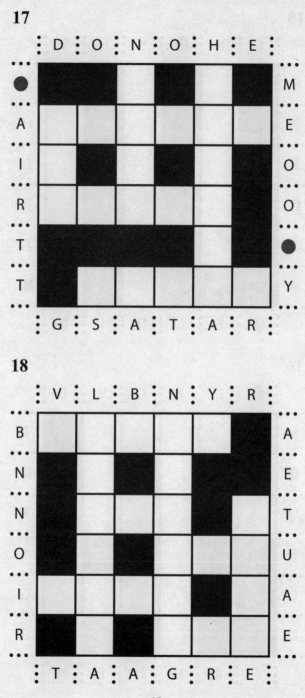

17

	D	O	N	O	H	E	
●							M
A							E
I							O
R							O
T							●
T							Y
	G	S	A	T	A	R	

18

	V	L	B	N	Y	R	
B							A
N							E
N							T
O							U
I							A
R							E
	T	A	A	G	R	E	

19

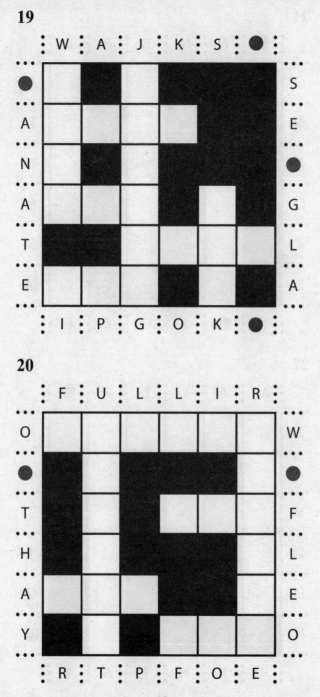

20

21

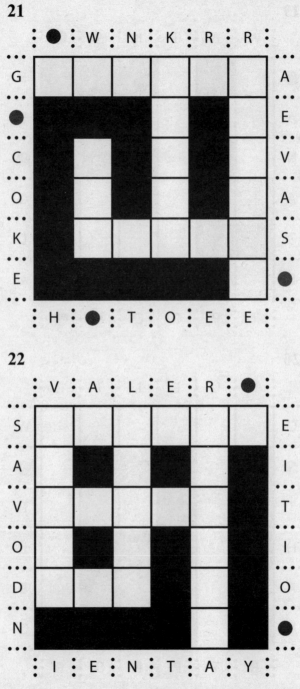

22

23

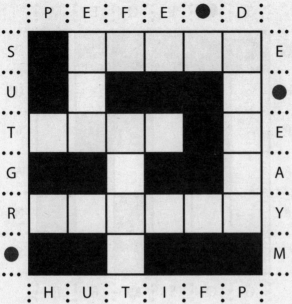

24

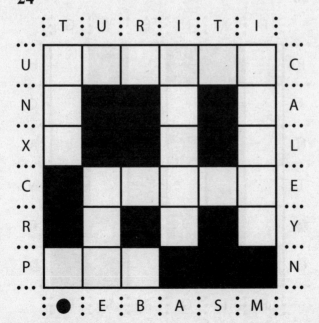

25

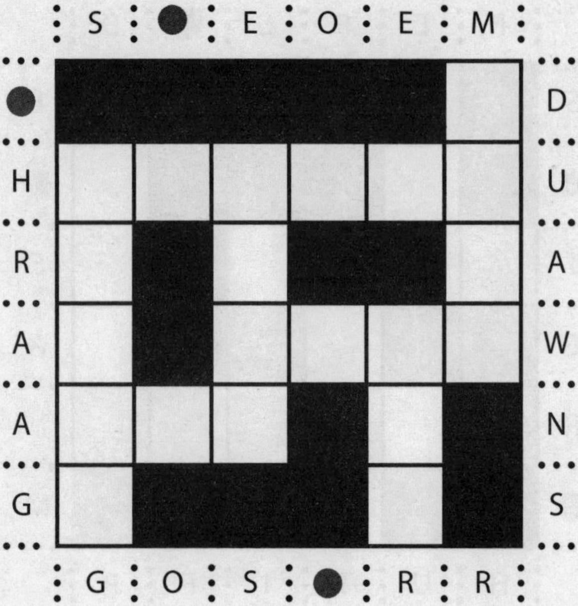
S ● E O E M
● H R A A G
D U A W N S
G O S ● R R

26

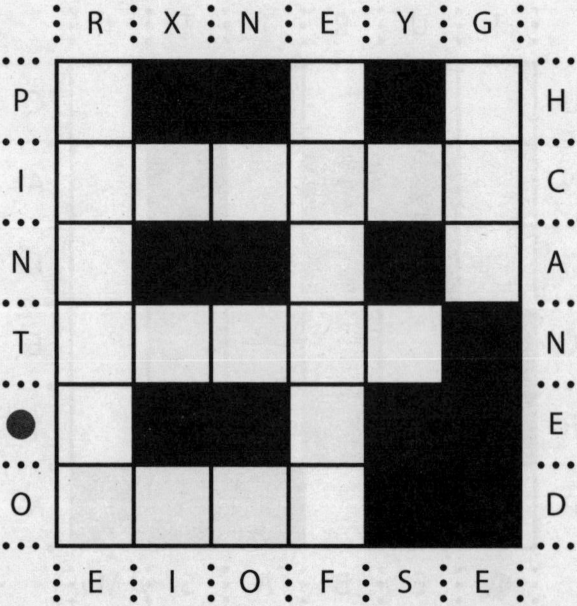
R X N E Y G
P I N T ● O
H C A N E D
E I O F S E

27

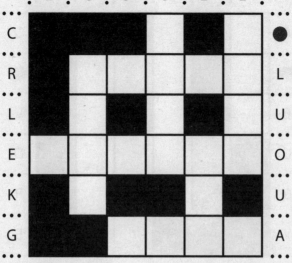

28

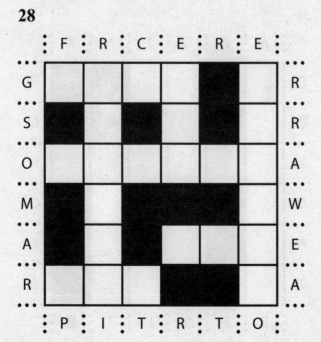

23

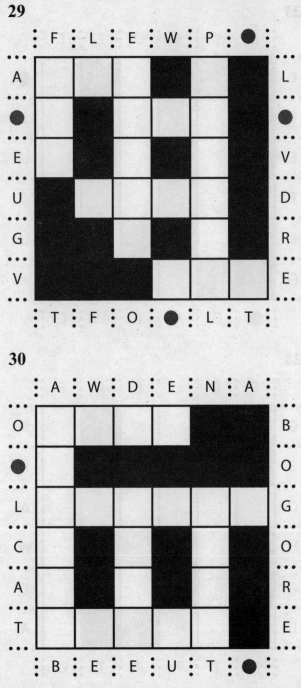

29

30

31

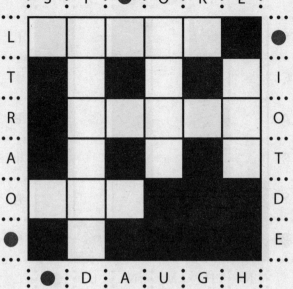

32

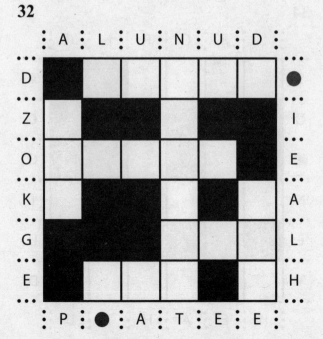

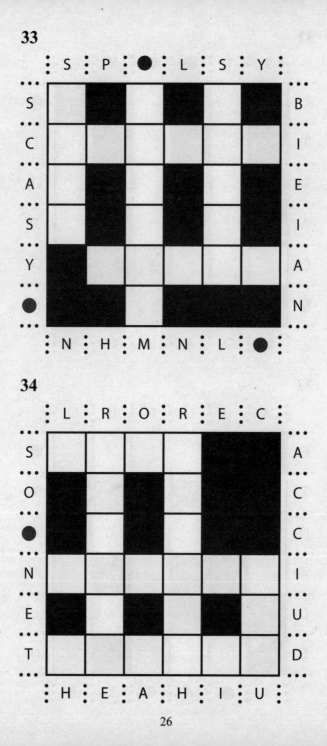

33

Top: S P ● L S Y

Left: S C A S Y ●

Right: B I E I A N

Bottom: N H M N L ●

34

Top: L R O R E C

Left: S O ● N E T

Right: A C C I U D

Bottom: H E A H I U

35

36

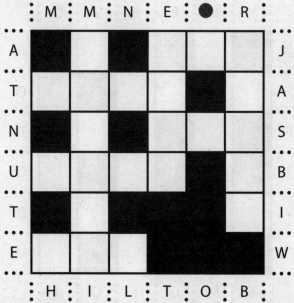

37

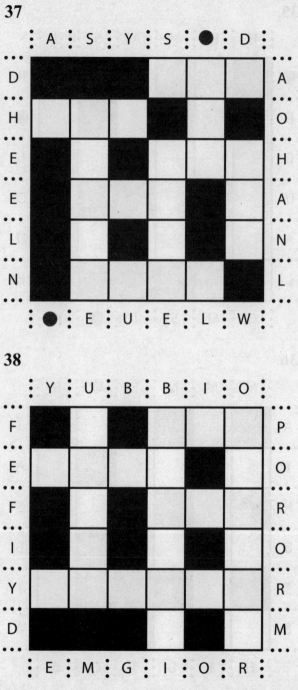

38

39

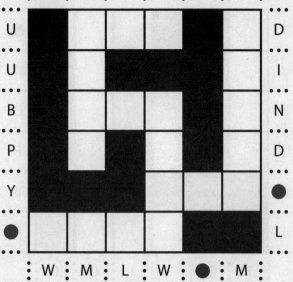

40

41

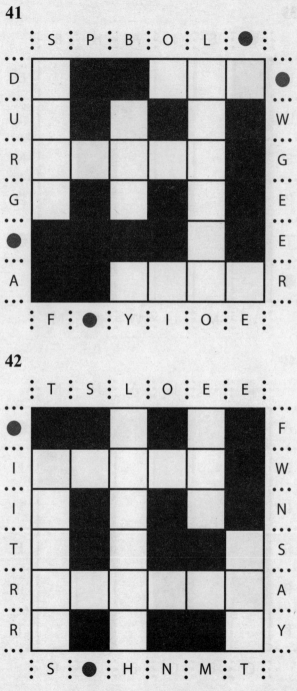

42

43

44

31

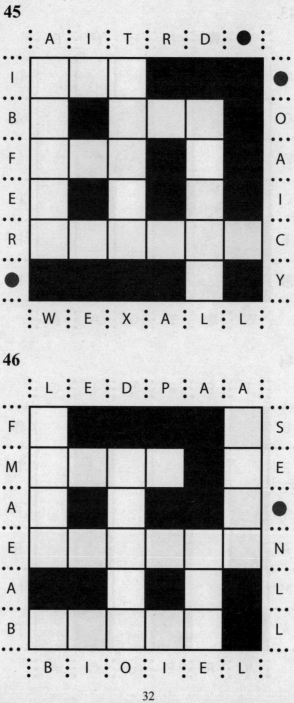

45

46

47

	A	N	K	E	W	E	
P							F
E							S
E							S
T							E
A							E
							C
	U	I	P	F	L	K	

48

	T	S	U	M	L	A	
Y							L
O							I
A							E
T							E
I							M
K							E
	A	P	E	L	A	M	

33

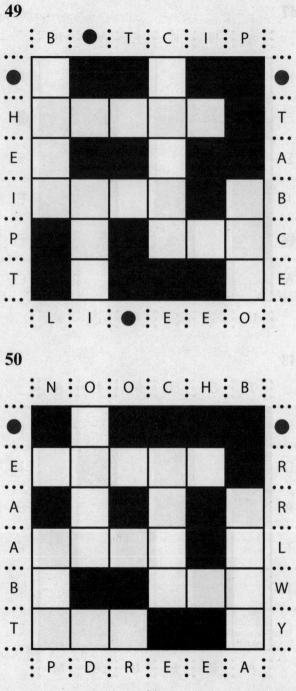

49

50

51

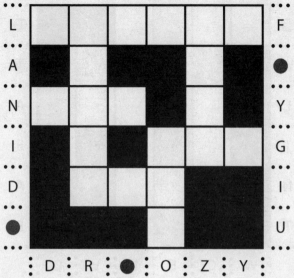

52

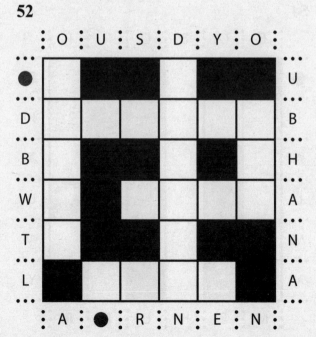

35

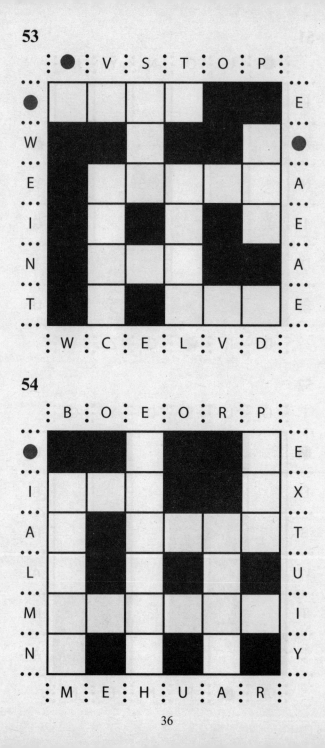

53

54

55

```
    C   O   R       A   I   D
P               ⬜
●                   ⬛          F
H       ⬛                      O
I       ⬛                      S
N               ⬛      ⬛      E
E   ⬛                          N
    ●   E   A   L   F   E
```

56

```
    E   E   T   E   E   N
H                              A
E   ⬛      ⬛      ⬛          M
R       ⬛      ⬛      ⬛      W
S                              U
D   ⬛      ⬛          ⬛      S
C   ⬛                          K
    ●   N   P   P   I   E
```

57

	B	B	●	A	I	T	
P							C
I							L
N							I
L							M
A							R
E							●
	S	U	A	G	E	D	

58

	D	A	R	W	D	N	
T							S
O							A
J							L
U							O
E							I
N							U
	V	I	W	I	A	G	

59

```
    C   R   S   O   L   D
P                           U
O                           A
U                           I
U                           R
T                           G
    B   I   L   B   E   Y
```

60

```
    H   A   X   A   E   Y
L                           N
X                           A
L                           M
A                           T
C                           L
K                           O
    F   E   R   S   O   T
```

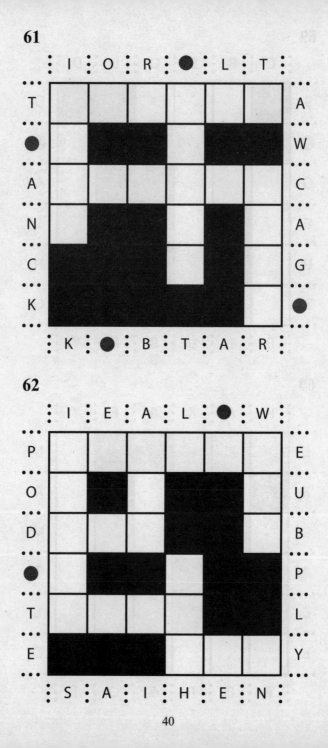

61

Top: I O R ● L T

Left: T ● A N C K

Right: A W C A G ●

Bottom: K ● B T A R

62

Top: I E A L ● W

Left: P O D ● T E

Right: E U B P L Y

Bottom: S A I H E N

63

Top: R ● A K S Y
Left: S ● D E R E
Right: U O I O N T
Bottom: E O M T N O

64

Top: D E O U E A
Left: O B I M A B
Right: T A E V I E
Bottom: J O R V O R

65

66

42

67

68

43

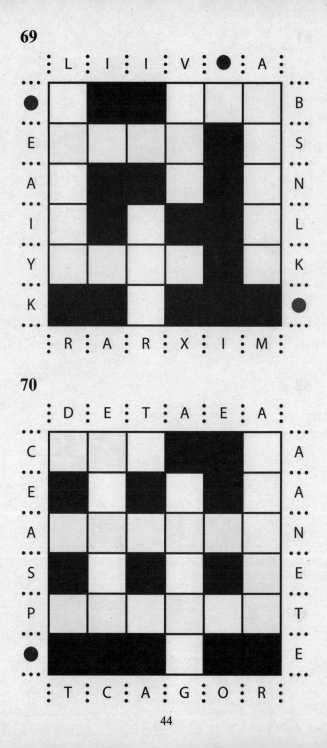

69

70

71

72

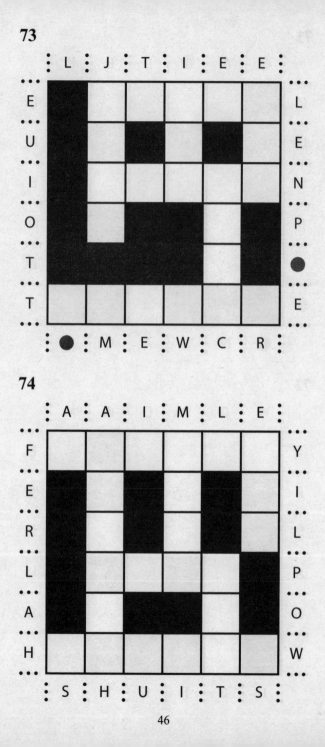

73

Across/Down letters:
- Top: L J T I E E
- Left: E U I O T T
- Right: L E N P E
- Bottom: M E W C R

74

Across/Down letters:
- Top: A A I M L E
- Left: F E R L A H
- Right: Y I L P O W
- Bottom: S H U I T S

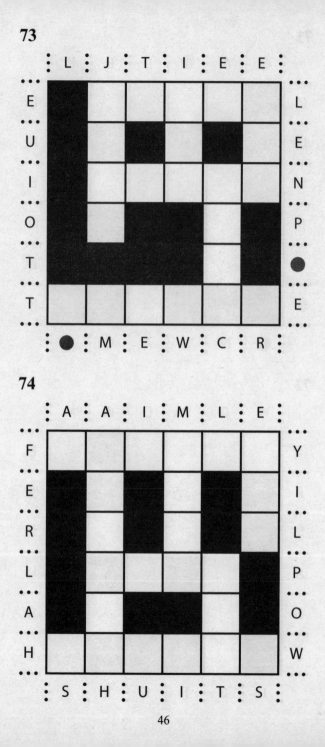

46

75

Top letters: ● D O P G B

Left letters: O ● D P O I

Right letters: C U L A ● N

Bottom letters: B N N O ● Y

76

Top letters: S A U I E G

Left letters: ● L L S E L

Right letters: G E S E ● P

Bottom letters: H S X L V T

47

75

Top: ● D O P G B
Left: O ● D P O I
Right: C U L A ● N
Bottom: B N N O ● Y

76

Top: S A U I E G
Left: ● L L S E L
Right: G E S E ● P
Bottom: H S X L V T

77

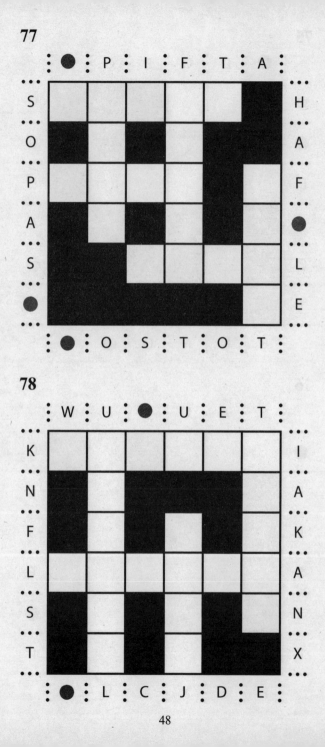

78

79

80

81

	●	L	I	B	S	T	
U							R
●							U
L							I
B							A
I							D
T							●
	G	B	H	A	N	R	

82

	O	I	N	O	L	T	
C							U
Y							O
E							L
E							P
N							E
T							D
	R	H	F	R	I	●	

50

83

Top: ● A R I D E
Left: W E K O ● E
Right: E H P E S Y
Bottom: Z W O E I G

84

Top: E U P S L I
Left: P I L A L T
Right: G E R I E E
Bottom: T E N M E L

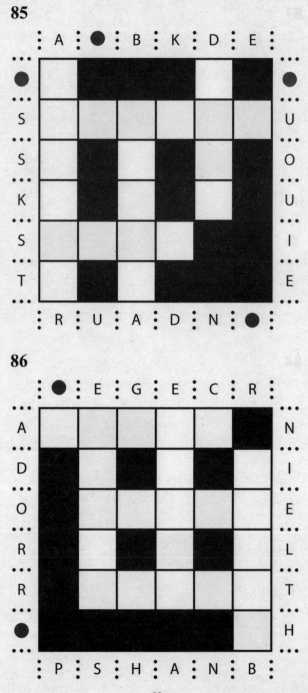

85

86

Lexica

Polygon

Quintagram®

Word Watch

Codeword

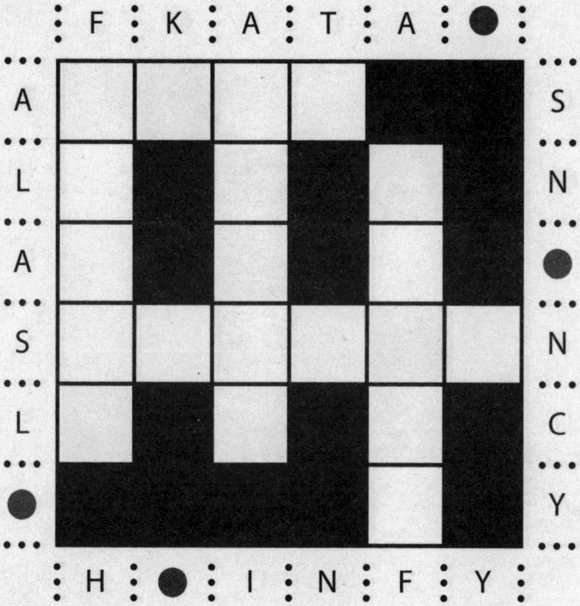

88

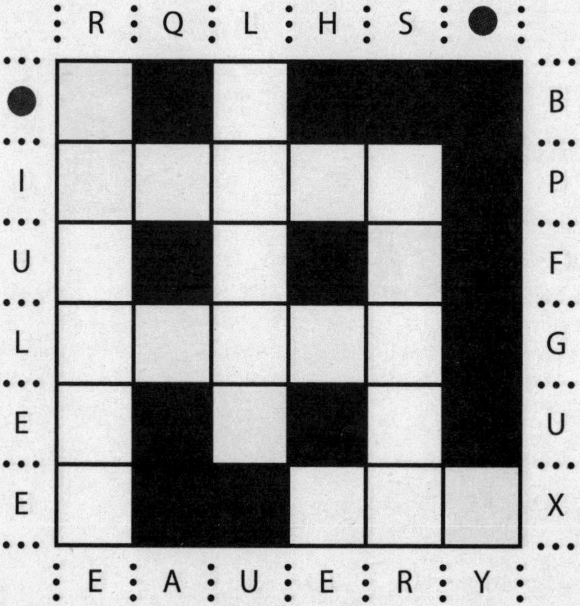

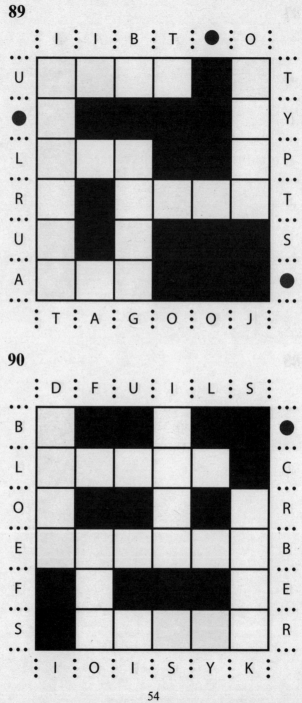

89

90

91

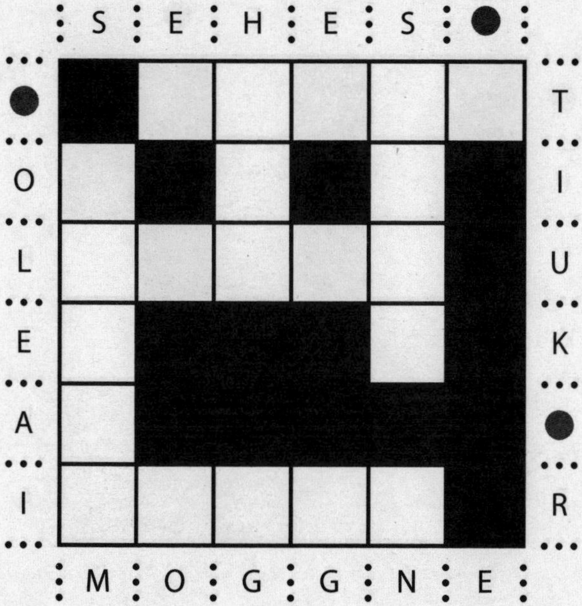

Top: S E H E S ●
Left: ● O L E A I
Right: T I U K ● R
Bottom: M O G G N E

92

Top: R O D L E O
Left: P M O U N D
Right: S D S T E E
Bottom: K I L E ● W

55

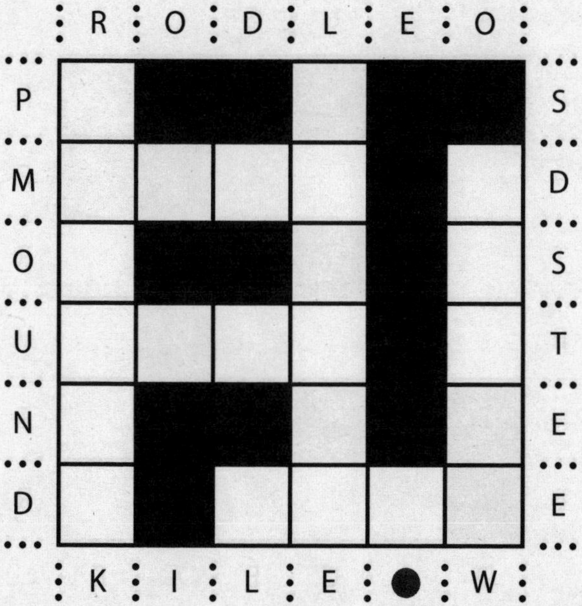

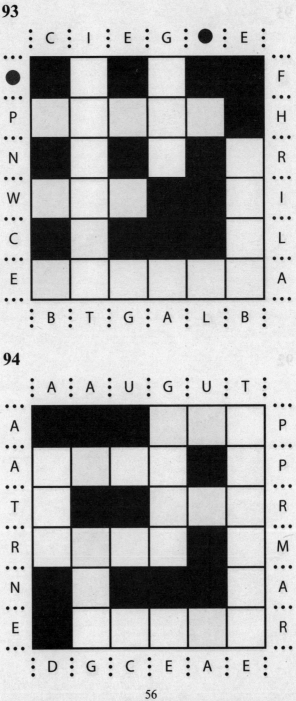

93

94

95

96

57

97

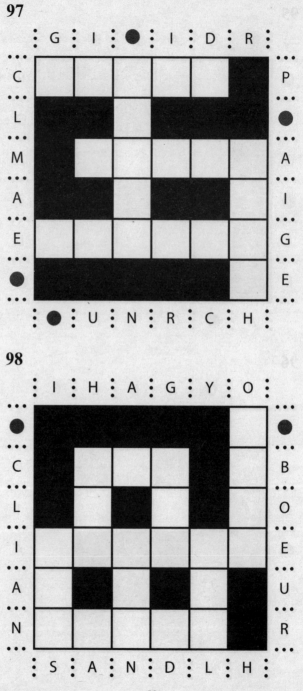

98

58

99

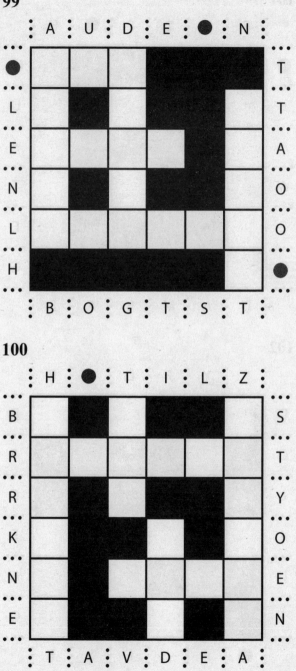

Top: A U D E ● N
Left: ● L E N L H
Right: T T A O O ●
Bottom: B O G T S T

100

Top: H ● T I L Z
Left: B R R K N E
Right: S T Y O E N
Bottom: T A V D E A

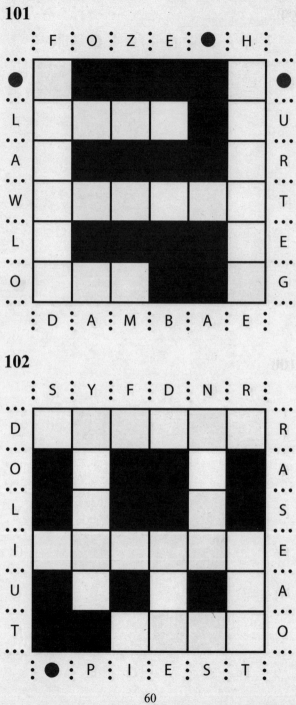

101

Top: F O Z E ● H

Left (top to bottom): ● L A W L O

Right (top to bottom): ● U R T E G

Bottom: D A M B A E

102

Top: S Y F D N R

Left (top to bottom): D O L I U T

Right (top to bottom): R A S E A O

Bottom: ● P I E S T

60

103

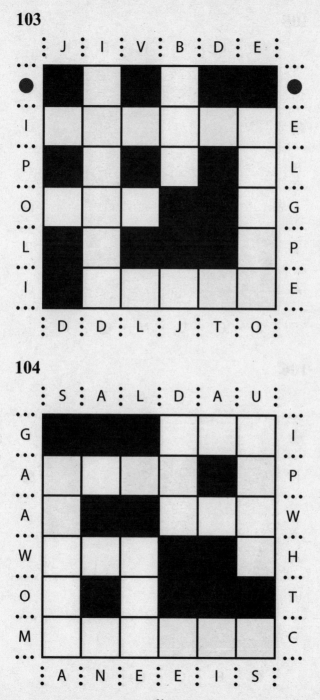

Top: J I V B D E
Left: I P O L I
Right: E L G P E
Bottom: D D L J T O

104

Top: S A L D A U
Left: G A A W O M
Right: I P W H T C
Bottom: A N E E I S

Lexica

Polygon

Quintagram®

Word Watch

Codeword

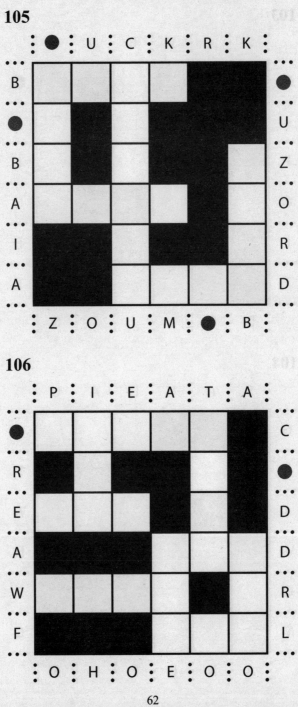

105

	●	U	C	K	R	K	
B							
●							U
B							Z
A							O
I							R
A							D
	Z	O	U	M	●	B	

106

	P	I	E	A	T	A	
●							C
R							●
E							D
A							D
W							R
F							L
	O	H	O	E	O	O	

Lexica · Polygon · Quintagram® · Word Watch · Codeword

62

107

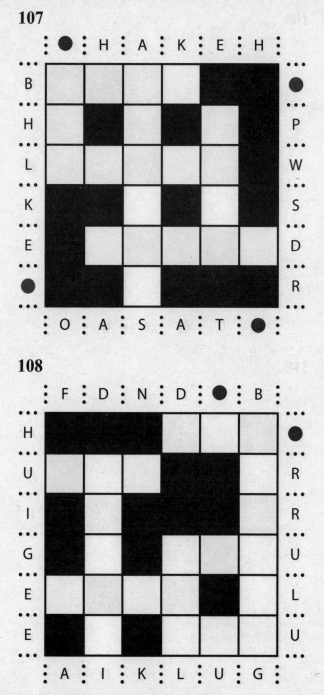

108

109

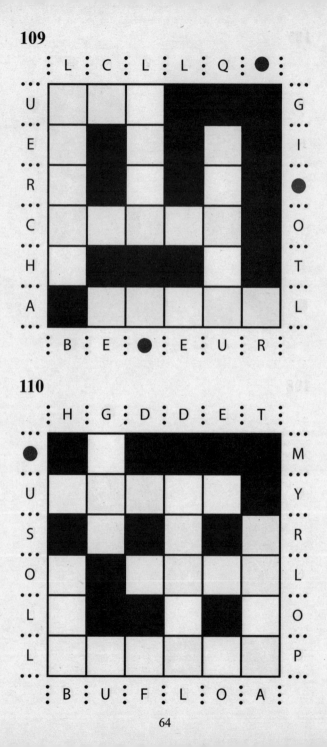

110

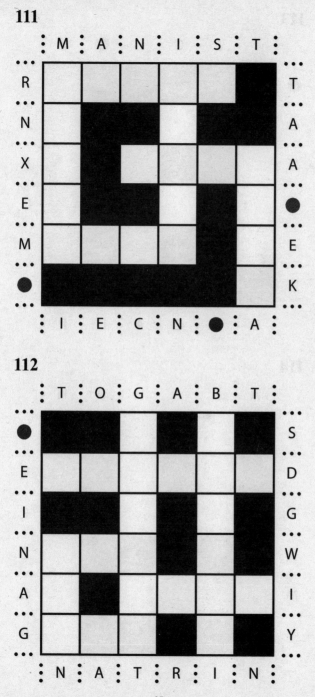

111

112

Lexica

Polygon

Quintagram®

Word Watch

Codeword

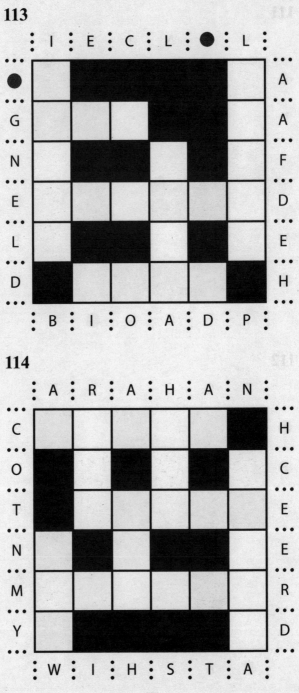

113

114

115

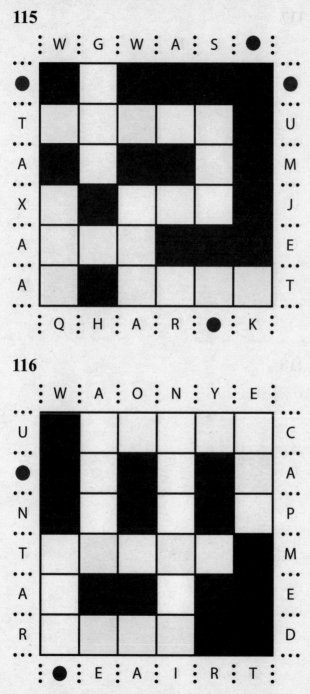

116

67

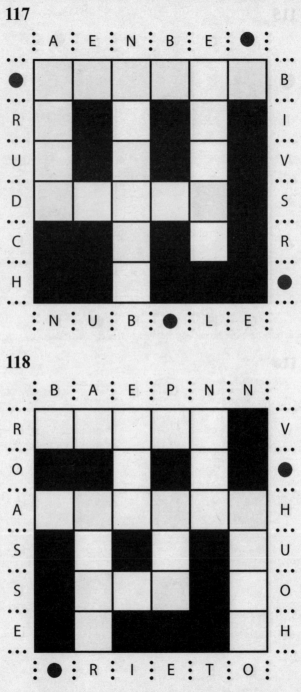

117

118

Lexica

Polygon

Quintagram®

Word Watch

Codeword

68

119

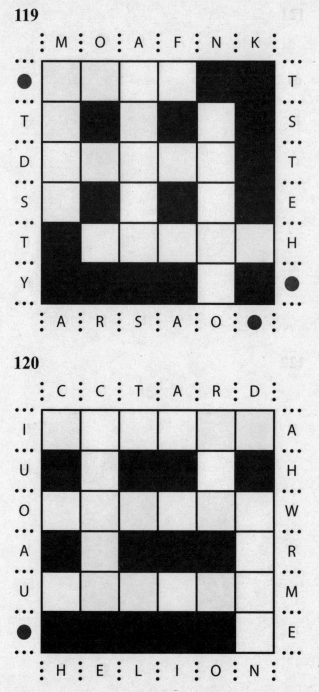

120

69

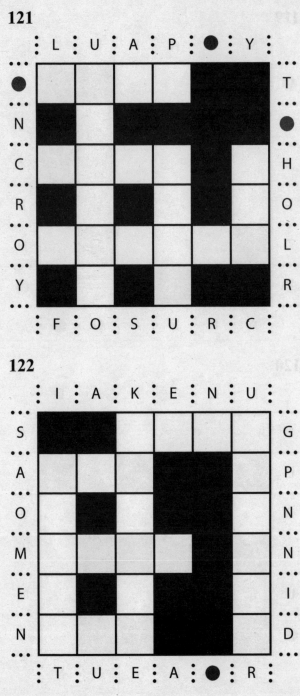

121

```
    L   U   A   P       ●   Y
●                           T
N                           ●
C                           H
R                           O
O                           L
Y                           R
    F   O   S   U   R   C
```

122

```
    I   A   K   E   N   U
S                           G
A                           P
O                           N
M                           N
E                           I
N                           D
    T   U   E   A   ●   R
```

70

123

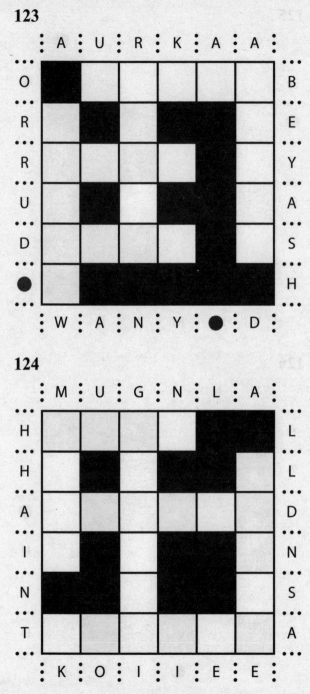

124

125

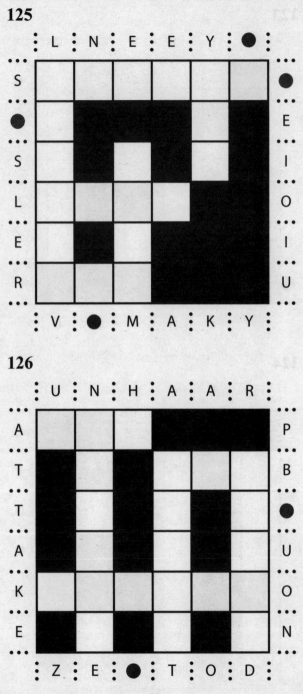

126

72

127

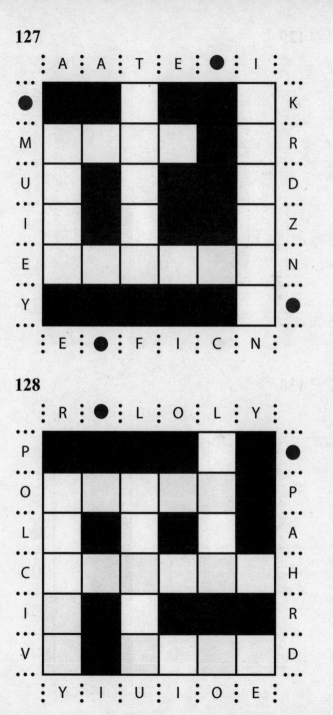

128

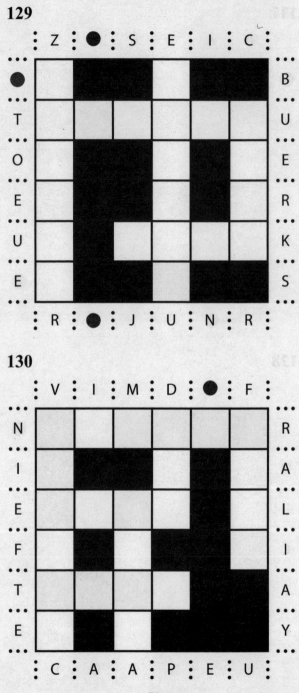

129

Top: Z ● S E I C

Left: ● T O E U E

Right: B U E R K S

Bottom: R ● J U N R

130

Top: V I M D ● F

Left: N I E F T E

Right: R A L I A Y

Bottom: C A A P E U

Lexica · Polygon · Quintagram® · Word Watch · Codeword

74

131

Top: ● H L E E R

Left: ● R C S R Y

Right: C O K T C ●

Bottom: S U E I P Y

132

Top: M E A N E R

Left: E V C I S S

Right: ● H A V N D

Bottom: B S W K O E

Polygon

Quintagram®

Word Watch

Codeword

133

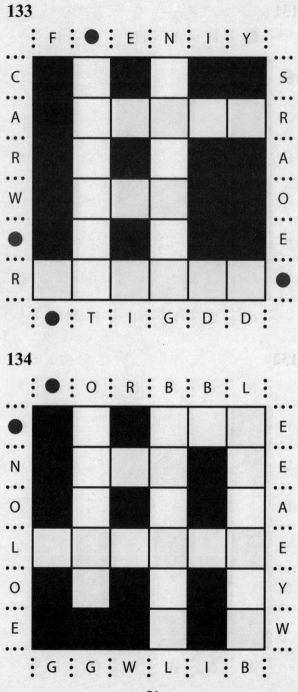

134

135

	●	L	A	I	I	C	
●							T
C							E
A							P
K							R
G						●	
C							I
	F	R	T	T	O	●	

136

	D	U	E	W	E	R	
T							S
A							H
●							A
S							P
A							E
P							N
	●	R	G	A	I	T	

137

```
      B   U   H   T   E   ●
   ┌───────────────────────┐
F  │███████████████████│   │ ●
   │───────────────────│   │
R  │   │   │   │   │   │   │ T
   │───│███│   │   │   │───│
U  │   │███│   │   │███│   │ O
   │───│   │───│███│   │───│
S  │   │   │   │███│   │   │ E
   │───│███│   │███│   │───│
M  │   │███│   │███│   │   │ K
   │───│   │   │   │███│───│
E  │███│   │   │   │███│███│ T
   └───────────────────────┘
      K   G   E   M   ●   C
```

138

```
      A   L   C   U   R   D
   ┌───────────────────────┐
G  │   │███│███│███│   │███│ ●
   │───│   │   │   │   │───│
B  │   │   │   │   │   │   │ S
   │───│███│   │   │███│───│
A  │   │███│   │   │███│███│ N
   │███│   │   │   │   │───│
N  │███│   │   │   │   │   │ I
   │───│   │███│   │   │───│
G  │███│   │███│   │   │   │ L
   │───│   │   │   │   │───│
L  │   │   │   │   │   │   │ D
   └───────────────────────┘
      B   E   O   G   E   R
```

78

139

140

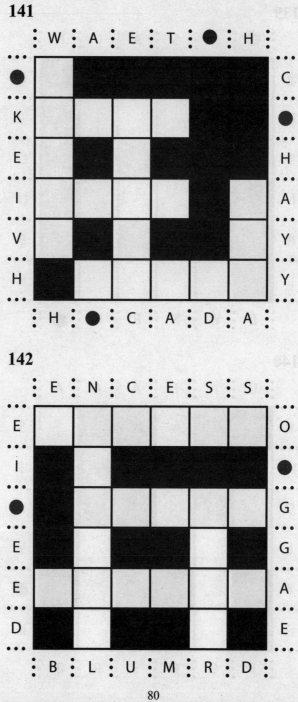

141

142

Lexica

Polygon

Quintagram®

Word Watch

Codeword

143

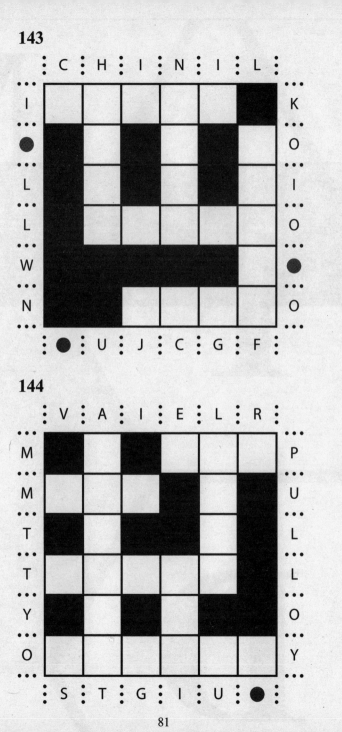

144

Lexica

Polygon

Quintagram®

Word Watch

Codeword

81

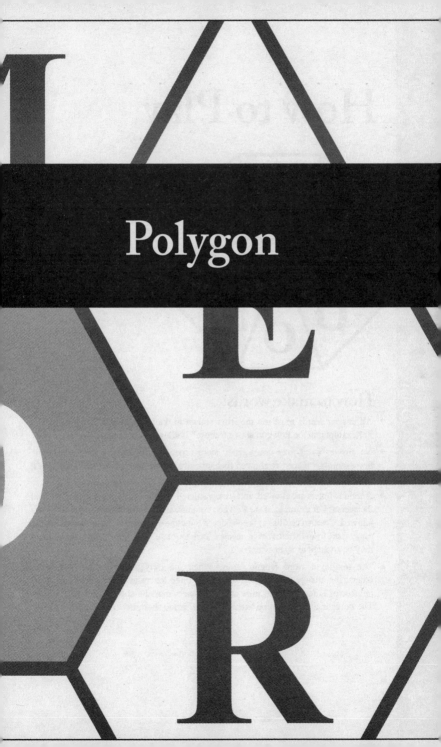

Polygon

How to Play

How to make words:

- All answer words must use the letter shown in the centre of the Polygon puzzle. For example, in the Polygon above, "noose" is allowed, but "moose" isn't.

- No answer word may use a letter more times than it appears in the Polygon. For example, "niece" is allowed (because two Es are given), but "concise" isn't, because there's only one C.

- Accented letters are allowed, and are considered identical to the same letters without the accent. For example, if the Polygon contains an E, words containing é, è or ê are allowed. C with a cedilla (ç) is considered the same as a plain C. If two words are the same apart from differences in accents, such as "pate" and "pâté", only one of them may be counted as an answer.

- The minimum word length varies. When the Polygon has a total of seven letters, the answer words must be at least three letters in length. When the total number of letters is eight, nine or ten, answers must be at least four letters long. The Polygon above has nine letters, so "con" is too short, but "icon" is allowed.

Acceptability of words:

- All answer words must be entries in the latest edition of the *Concise Oxford English Dictionary* (COED). The 12th edition was published in 2011.

- Answer words must be listed in COED without capital letters. For example, "Moonie" and "Miocene" aren't allowed.

- Answers must be listed in COED as single words, without hyphens or other punctuation such as apostrophes. For example, "come on" and "come-on" aren't allowed, and "amino" isn't allowed because COED has it only in the phrase "amino acid".

- Plural nouns aren't allowed, even if they're irregularly formed. For example, "coins", "monies" and "icemen" aren't allowed. However, if a plural noun is explicitly listed in COED as a different part of speech, it is allowed. For example, "forwards" (adverb) and "crumbs" (exclamation) are allowed.

- Only the base forms of verbs are allowed (the infinitive, without the word "to"), not any variations such as present tense, past tense or participles, even if they're irregularly formed. For example, "see" is allowed, but not "sees", "seeing" or "seen". However, if a verb form is explicitly listed in COED as a different part of speech, it is allowed. For example, "saw" (noun), "learned" (adjective) and "given" (adjective, preposition or noun) are allowed.

- Agent nouns ending in -er are allowed if they're listed in COED. For example, "mincer" is allowed, but "mooner" isn't.

- Basic forms of adjectives are allowed, but not comparatives (usually ending in -er) or superlatives (usually ending in -est). For example, "nice" is allowed, but "nicer" and "nicest" aren't. Irregular comparatives and superlatives such as "better", "best" and "worse" are disallowed as forms of adjectives, but many of them are also listed in COED as other parts of speech (eg "worst" = "get the better of"), and are therefore allowed on that basis.

- Adverbs ending in -ly aren't allowed.

  Any word in COED is allowed, even if it's marked as slang, archaic, US, etc.

- Occasionally, you may find words that fit all the above criteria but aren't listed among the printed answers. If you do, you can feel satisfied that you've outwitted the puzzle setter.

Hints for solving:

- Look for common beginnings, such as UN- or SUB-, and endings, such as -ER or -ISM. Look for pairs of letters that go well together, such as ST, PR or ND.

- Write out the letters in a different order, in case you spot something different.

- Don't forget to look for words that begin with a vowel.

  When you find a word, try reading it backwards, to see if it suggests another word.

- When you find a word, try to find all the rearrangements of its letters that also form words.

- When you find a word, try substituting the remaining letters into it.

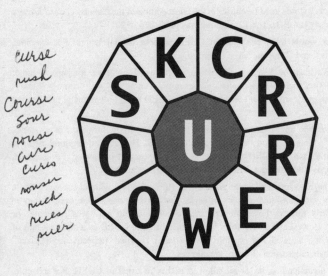

1

curse
push
course
sour
rouse
cure
cures
rouser
ruck
rules
ruler

2

flan
hand
haul
froad
faun
bland
land
half
had
lad
fan

3

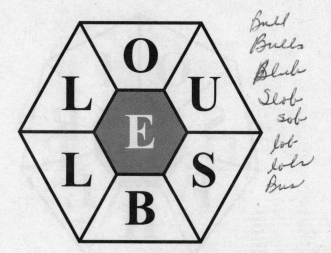

Bull
Bulls
Bulb
Slob
Sob
lob
lobs
Bus

4

gin
mage
mene
imagine
cige
name
mean
game
gem

5

6

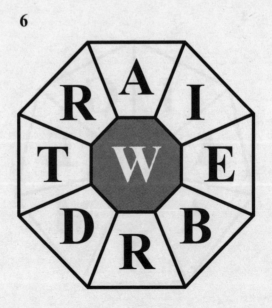

7

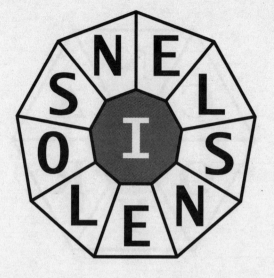

8

9

10

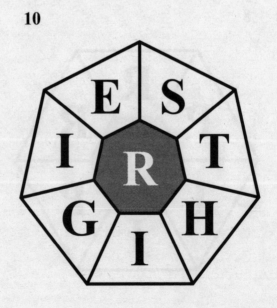

Lexica

Polygon

Quintagram®

Word Watch

Codeword

11

12

13

14

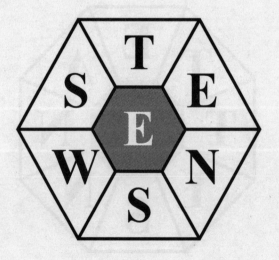

15

16

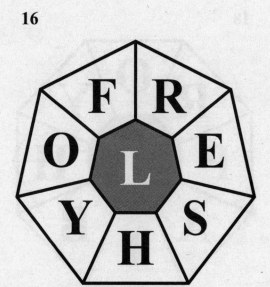

17

18

19

20

21

22

23

24

25

26

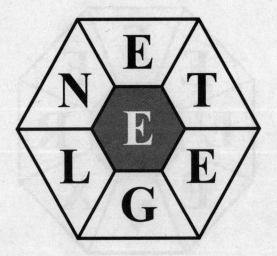

27

28

29

30

31

32

33

34

35

36

Lexica

Polygon

Quintagram®

Word Watch

Codeword

37

38

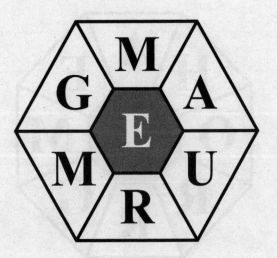

39

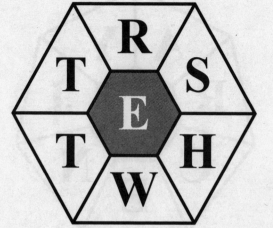

40

41

42

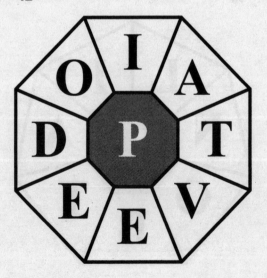

43

44

45

46

47

48

49

50

51

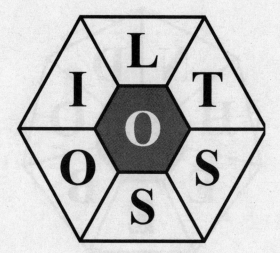

52

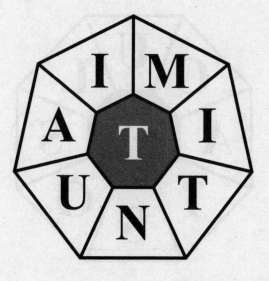

53

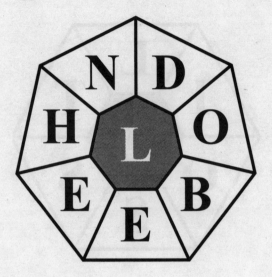

54

55

56

57

58

59

60

61

62

63

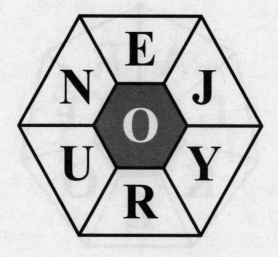

64

65

66

65

66

67

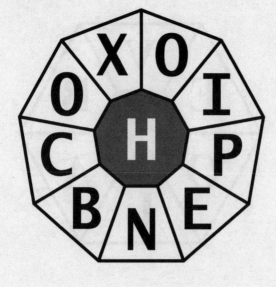

68

69

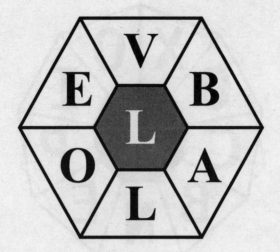

70

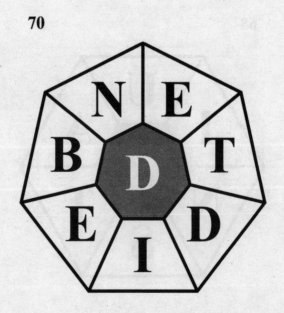

71

72

73

74

75

76

77

78

79

80

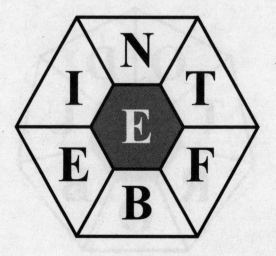

81

82

83

84

85

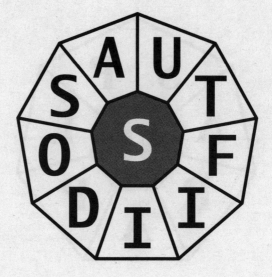

86

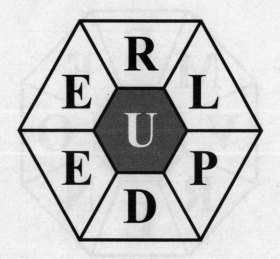

87

88

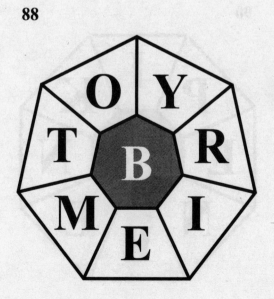

89

90

91

92

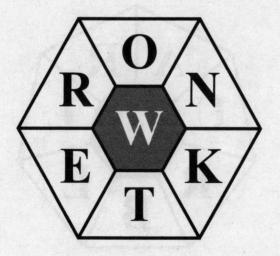

93

94

95

96

Lexica

Polygon

Quintagram®

Word Watch

Codeword

97

98

99

100

101

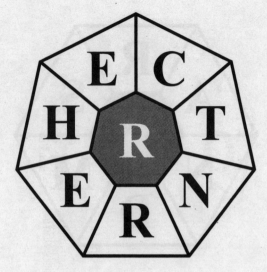

102

103

104

106

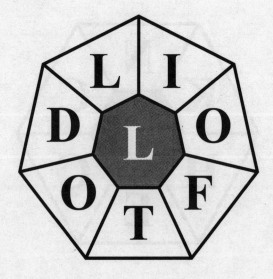

107

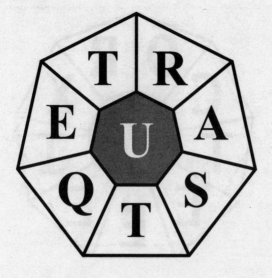

108

109

110

Lexica

Polygon

Quintagram®

Word Watch

Codeword

111

112

113

114

142

115

116

117

118

119

120

121

122

123

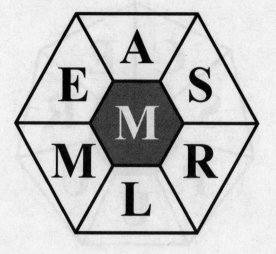

124

125

126

127

128

149

129

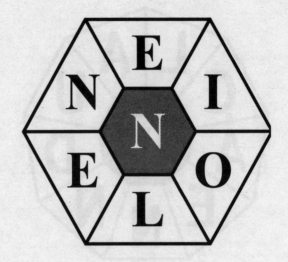

130

131

132

133

134

135

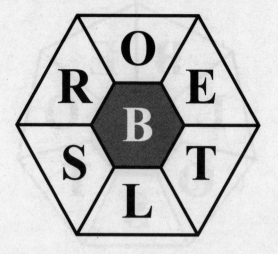

136

137

138

139

140

141

142

143

144

4 Playground ga

— — — — —

5 Second wife of

A	A	A	B
E	E	E	E
I	I	I	N

e (8)

_ _ _ _

enry VIII (4,6)

D	E	E	E
F	G	I	K
N	N	N	N

How to Play

Answer each clue in crossword fashion. Enter each answer in the spaces below its clue, and cross out the letters in the matrix at the bottom, as with GUST in the example. The puzzle is complete when every letter in the matrix is crossed out.

1 Sudden blast of wind (4)

_ _ _ _

2 Glossy fabric (5)

_ _ _ _ _

3 Tropical bird (6)

_ _ _ _ _ _

4 Trip, voyage (7)

_ _ _ _ _ _ _

5 Co-discoverer of radium (5,5)

_ _ _ _ _ _ _ _ _ _

A	A	A	C	E	E	E	G
I	I	I	J	M	N	N	O
O	P	R	R	R	R	R	S
S	T	T	T	U	U	U	Y

1 Sudden blast of wind (4)

_G_ _U_ _S_ _T_

2 Glossy fabric (5)

_ _ _ _ _

3 Tropical bird (6)

_ _ _ _ _ _

4 Trip, voyage (7)

_ _ _ _ _ _ _

5 Co-discoverer of radium (5,5)

_ _ _ _ _ _ _ _ _ _

A	A	A	C	E	E	E	~~G~~
I	I	I	J	M	N	N	O
O	P	R	R	R	R	R	~~S~~
S	~~T~~	T	T	~~U~~	U	U	Y

1

1 First appearance (5)

_ _ _ _ _

2 French artist (5)

_ _ _ _ _

3 Concealed (6)

_ _ _ _ _ _

4 Handbook (6)

_ _ _ _ _ _

5 Common British butterfly (3,7)

_ _ _ _ _ _ _ _ _ _

A	A	A	A	B	D	D	D
D	D	E	E	E	E	H	I
I	L	L	M	M	M	N	N
N	O	R	R	T	T	U	U

2

1 Confidence trick (4)

_ _ _ _

2 Texan city (6)

_ _ _ _ _ _

3 Deep shade of red (7)

_ _ _ _ _ _ _

4 Suggest, put forward (7)

_ _ _ _ _ _ _

5 Explanatory list of terms (8)

_ _ _ _ _ _ _ _

A	A	A	A	C	C	D	E
G	I	L	L	L	M	M	N
O	O	O	O	P	P	R	R
R	S	S	S	S	S	S	Y

Concise Quintagrams®

3

1 Test of knowledge (4)

_ _ _ _

2 Madagascan primate (5)

_ _ _ _ _

3 In recent times (6)

_ _ _ _ _ _

4 Treasure, hold dear (7)

_ _ _ _ _ _ _

5 *Paradise Lost* poet (4,6)

_ _ _ _ _ _ _ _ _ _

A	C	E	E	E	H	H	H
I	I	I	J	L	L	L	L
M	M	N	N	O	O	Q	R
R	S	T	T	U	U	Y	Z

4

1 Melt (4)

_ _ _ _

2 Rough, grating (5)

_ _ _ _ _

3 Human mind (6)

_ _ _ _ _ _

4 English county (7)

_ _ _ _ _ _ _

5 Thigh muscle (10)

_ _ _ _ _ _ _ _ _ _

A	A	A	C	C	D	E	E
F	H	H	H	H	I	K	L
N	O	O	P	P	Q	R	R
R	S	S	S	T	U	W	Y

Lexica

Polygon

Quintagram®

Word Watch

Codeword

Concise Quintagrams®

5

1 Stylish (4)

_ _ _ _

2 Tropical fruit (5)

_ _ _ _ _

3 Unit of work (5)

_ _ _ _ _

4 Victimise (9)

_ _ _ _ _ _ _ _ _

5 Tribal leader (9)

_ _ _ _ _ _ _ _ _

A	A	C	C	C	C	E	E
E	E	E	F	G	H	H	I
I	I	J	L	M	N	N	O
O	P	R	S	T	T	U	U

6

1 Andean country (5)

_ _ _ _ _

2 Standoffish, supercilious (5)

_ _ _ _ _

3 Spotted big cat (6)

_ _ _ _ _ _

4 Baffled (7)

_ _ _ _ _ _ _

5 Former poet laureate (3,6)

_ _ _ _ _ _ _ _ _

A	A	A	C	D	D	E	E
E	E	F	G	G	H	H	H
I	J	L	L	M	O	O	P
R	S	S	T	T	U	U	U

Concise Quintagrams®

7

1 Supplant, expel (4)

_ _ _ _

2 Island in the Aegean Sea (6)

_ _ _ _ _ _

3 Ten-legged creature (7)

_ _ _ _ _ _ _

4 Luck (7)

_ _ _ _ _ _ _

5 Common garden bird (5,3)

_ _ _ _ _ _ _ _

A	A	C	D	D	D	E	E
E	E	F	G	H	I	N	O
O	O	O	P	R	R	R	S
S	T	T	T	T	T	U	U

8

1 Nocturnal mammal (3)

_ _ _

2 Cruise ship (5)

_ _ _ _ _

3 Change, adjust (6)

_ _ _ _ _ _

4 Large gathering of Scouts (8)

_ _ _ _ _ _ _ _

5 Horticultural construction (10)

_ _ _ _ _ _ _ _ _ _

A	A	B	B	D	E	E	E
E	E	E	F	G	H	I	I
J	L	M	M	N	N	O	O
O	R	R	R	S	T	U	Y

Concise Quintagrams®

9

1 Group of sheep or birds (5)

_ _ _ _ _

2 Able to survive cold weather (5)

_ _ _ _ _

3 Curly-haired dog breed (6)

_ _ _ _ _ _

4 Compress (7)

_ _ _ _ _ _ _

5 Mouth organ (9)

_ _ _ _ _ _ _ _ _

A	A	A	C	C	D	D	E
E	E	E	F	H	H	I	K
L	L	M	N	O	O	O	O
P	Q	R	R	S	U	Y	Z

10

1 Female horse (4)

_ _ _ _

2 Boat propelled with a pole (4)

_ _ _ _

3 Put back to an initial state (5)

_ _ _ _ _

4 Widespread agreement (9)

_ _ _ _ _ _ _ _ _

5 Ziggy Stardust singer (5,5)

_ _ _ _ _ _ _ _ _ _

A	A	B	C	D	D	E	E
E	E	E	I	I	M	N	N
N	O	O	P	R	R	S	S
S	S	T	T	U	U	V	W

Concise Quintagrams®

166

11

1 Fizzy drinks (3)

_ _ _

2 Midwestern US state (4)

_ _ _ _

3 Publicity stunt (7)

_ _ _ _ _ _ _

4 Imperil (8)

_ _ _ _ _ _ _ _

5 Peerless Australian cricketer (3,7)

_ _ _ _ _ _ _ _ _ _

A	A	A	A	B	C	D	D
D	E	E	G	G	I	I	I
K	M	M	M	N	N	N	N
O	O	O	P	P	R	R	W

12

1 Ensemble of actors (4)

_ _ _ _

2 Slender, restricted (6)

_ _ _ _ _ _

3 High-spirited behaviour (6)

_ _ _ _ _ _

4 Front tooth (7)

_ _ _ _ _ _ _

5 Large sea bird (9)

_ _ _ _ _ _ _ _ _

A	A	A	A	A	B	C	C
C	I	I	I	L	N	N	N
O	O	O	R	R	R	R	S
S	S	S	S	T	T	T	W

Concise Quintagrams®

167

13

1 Courtroom panel (4)

_ _ _ _

2 Competitor (5)

_ _ _ _ _

3 Crush underfoot (7)

_ _ _ _ _ _ _

4 Thin and bony (7)

_ _ _ _ _ _ _

5 Scottish engineer (5,4)

_ _ _ _ _ _ _ _ _

A	A	A	A	A	C	E	E
I	J	J	L	L	M	M	N
P	R	R	R	R	S	S	T
T	T	U	V	W	W	Y	Y

14

1 Clock face (4)

_ _ _ _

2 Enthusiastic, eager (4)

_ _ _ _

3 Britain's longest river (6)

_ _ _ _ _ _

4 Playground game (8)

_ _ _ _ _ _ _ _

5 Second wife of Henry VIII (4,6)

_ _ _ _ _ _ _ _ _ _

A	A	A	B	D	E	E	E
E	E	E	E	F	G	I	K
L	L	L	N	N	N	N	N
O	O	P	R	R	S	V	Y

Concise Quintagrams®

15

1 Clarified butter (4)

_ _ _ _

2 Ready for sleep (6)

_ _ _ _ _ _

3 Not liable for tax (6)

_ _ _ _ _ _

4 Baltic country (7)

_ _ _ _ _ _ _

5 Wealth, prosperity (9)

_ _ _ _ _ _ _ _ _

A	A	C	D	E	E	E	E
E	E	E	F	F	G	H	I
L	M	N	N	O	O	P	R
S	S	T	T	U	W	X	Y

16

1 Menagerie (3)

_ _ _

2 Greek goddess of victory (4)

_ _ _ _

3 *Peter Grimes* composer (7)

_ _ _ _ _ _ _

4 Divine prediction (8)

_ _ _ _ _ _ _ _

5 Unbeatable (10)

_ _ _ _ _ _ _ _ _ _

B	B	C	C	E	E	E	E
H	I	I	I	I	I	K	L
N	N	N	N	O	O	O	P
P	R	R	T	T	V	Y	Z

Polygon

Quintagram®

Word Watch

Codeword

Concise Quintagrams®

Polygon

Quintagram®

Word Watch

Codeword

17

1 Milk supplier (5)

_ _ _ _ _

2 Saying on a coat of arms (5)

_ _ _ _ _

3 Select, opt (6)

_ _ _ _ _ _

4 Cumbrian market town (7)

_ _ _ _ _ _ _

5 Jazz instrument (9)

_ _ _ _ _ _ _ _ _

A	A	C	C	D	E	E	E
H	H	I	I	K	K	M	N
O	O	O	O	O	O	P	R
S	S	S	T	T	W	X	Y

18

1 Poem such as the *Iliad* (4)

_ _ _ _

2 Allege (5)

_ _ _ _ _

3 Arboreal ape (6)

_ _ _ _ _ _

4 Combination (7)

_ _ _ _ _ _ _

5 Author of *Persuasion* (4,6)

_ _ _ _ _ _ _ _ _ _

A	A	A	B	B	C	C	E
E	E	E	G	I	I	I	I
J	L	M	M	N	N	N	O
P	R	S	T	T	U	U	X

Concise Quintagrams®

19

1 Bovine beast of burden (3)

_ _ _

2 Conspiracy (4)

_ _ _ _

3 Shake, tremble (6)

_ _ _ _ _ _

4 Electronic component (9)

_ _ _ _ _ _ _ _ _

5 Lover of fine cuisine (10)

_ _ _ _ _ _ _ _ _ _

A	A	C	C	E	E	G	H
I	I	I	K	L	M	M	N
O	O	O	O	P	P	Q	R
R	R	S	T	T	U	V	Y

20

1 Move about restlessly (6)

_ _ _ _ _ _

2 Cracow's country (6)

_ _ _ _ _ _

3 Islamic place of worship (6)

_ _ _ _ _ _

4 Traditional drinking vessel (7)

_ _ _ _ _ _ _

5 Marine mammal (7)

_ _ _ _ _ _ _

A	A	A	D	D	D	D	E
E	F	G	H	I	I	K	L
L	M	N	N	N	O	O	O
P	P	Q	R	S	T	T	U

Concise Quintagrams®

21

1 Rage (4)

— — — —

2 Imperial unit of weight (5)

— — — — —

3 Edible shellfish (7)

— — — — — — —

4 Bunch together in a group (7)

— — — — — — —

5 Covering for the eyes (9)

— — — — — — — — —

A	B	C	C	C	D	D	E
E	F	F	I	L	L	L	L
L	N	N	O	O	O	P	R
R	S	S	T	U	U	U	Y

22

1 Labyrinth (4)

— — — —

2 Sword handle (4)

— — — —

3 Agricultural implement (6)

— — — — — —

4 Tea flavoured with bergamot (4,4)

— — — — — — — —

5 Diverging from convention (10)

— — — — — — — — — —

A	A	D	E	E	E	G	G
H	H	H	I	L	L	L	M
N	O	O	O	O	P	R	R
R	T	T	U	U	X	Y	Z

Concise Quintagrams®

23

1 Coloured liquid for staining (3)

_ _ _

2 West African country (5)

_ _ _ _ _

3 Dietary essential found in meat (7)

_ _ _ _ _ _ _

4 Copy (7)

_ _ _ _ _ _ _

5 Birdwatching aid (10)

_ _ _ _ _ _ _ _ _ _

A	A	A	A	B	C	D	E
E	E	G	H	I	I	I	I
L	M	N	N	N	O	O	P
R	R	S	T	T	T	U	Y

24

1 Minor piece in chess (4)

_ _ _ _

2 Adjust slightly (5)

_ _ _ _ _

3 Open-toed shoe (6)

_ _ _ _ _ _

4 Tree producing may blossom (8)

_ _ _ _ _ _ _ _

5 *To Kill a Mockingbird* author (6,3)

_ _ _ _ _ _ _ _ _

A	A	A	A	A	A	D	E
E	E	E	H	H	H	K	L
L	N	N	N	O	P	P	R
R	R	S	T	T	W	W	W

Concise Quintagrams®

173

25

1 Morose, gloomy (4)

— — — —

2 Literary category (5)

— — — — —

3 Limp (6)

— — — — — —

4 Plant's curling shoot (7)

— — — — — — —

5 Newest UK national park (5,5)

— — — — — — — — — —

B	B	D	D	D	E	E	E
E	G	H	H	I	L	L	N
N	N	O	O	O	O	R	R
R	S	S	T	T	U	U	W

26

1 Evergreen climbing plant (3)

— — —

2 Short-lived fashion (5)

— — — — —

3 Trumpet flourish (7)

— — — — — — —

4 Easy to read (7)

— — — — — — —

5 Shakespeare play (3,7)

— — — — — — — — — —

A	A	A	B	C	E	E	E
E	E	E	E	F	F	G	H
I	I	L	L	M	N	P	R
R	S	T	T	T	V	Y	Z

Concise Quintagrams®

174

27

1 Jump (4)

_ _ _ _

2 Walled city of N England (4)

_ _ _ _

3 Strong, concentrated (6)

_ _ _ _ _ _

4 Rocky celestial body (8)

_ _ _ _ _ _ _ _

5 Pickled cabbage (10)

_ _ _ _ _ _ _ _ _ _

A	A	A	A	D	E	E	E
E	I	K	K	L	N	O	O
O	P	P	R	R	R	R	S
S	T	T	T	T	U	U	Y

28

1 Taxi (3)

_ _ _

2 Weasel-like mammal (5)

_ _ _ _ _

3 Strike repeatedly with the fists (6)

_ _ _ _ _ _

4 Item of laboratory apparatus (4,4)

_ _ _ _ _ _ _ _

5 Celebrated singer-songwriter (4,6)

_ _ _ _ _ _ _ _ _ _

A	A	B	B	C	E	E	E
E	H	J	L	L	M	M	N
N	N	N	O	O	O	P	S
S	T	T	T	T	T	U	U

Concise Quintagrams®

29

1 Banded gemstone (4)

_ _ _ _

2 Displeased facial expression (5)

_ _ _ _ _

3 Tycoon (7)

_ _ _ _ _ _ _

4 Good-looking (8)

_ _ _ _ _ _ _ _

5 Second World War fighter plane (8)

_ _ _ _ _ _ _ _

A	A	A	D	E	E	E	F
F	G	H	I	I	M	M	N
N	N	N	O	O	O	P	R
R	S	S	T	T	W	X	Y

30

1 Innermost part, centre (4)

_ _ _ _

2 Doglike African carnivore (5)

_ _ _ _ _

3 Confuse, mix up (6)

_ _ _ _ _ _

4 Requiring hard graft (7)

_ _ _ _ _ _ _

5 Indecipherable jargon (5,5)

_ _ _ _ _ _ _ _ _ _

A	A	B	B	C	D	D	D
E	E	E	H	J	L	M	M
M	M	N	O	O	O	O	R
R	S	U	U	U	U	U	Y

Concise Quintagrams®

176

31

1 Curse, hoodoo (4)

_ _ _ _

2 Confronted (5)

_ _ _ _ _

3 Parrot's harsh call (6)

_ _ _ _ _ _

4 Statement expressing remorse (7)

_ _ _ _ _ _ _

5 Jewish coming-of-age ceremony (3,7)

_ _ _ _ _ _ _ _ _ _

A	A	A	A	A	B	C	D
E	F	G	H	I	I	J	K
L	M	N	O	O	P	Q	R
S	T	U	V	W	X	Y	Z

32

1 Gentle, lacking intensity (4)

_ _ _ _

2 Raise (a flag, eg) (5)

_ _ _ _ _

3 Repeated section of a song (6)

_ _ _ _ _ _

4 Trailblazer (7)

_ _ _ _ _ _ _

5 Early Victorian novelist (4,6)

_ _ _ _ _ _ _ _ _ _

A	B	C	D	E	E	E	E
H	H	I	I	I	L	M	N
N	N	N	O	O	O	O	P
R	R	R	S	S	T	T	U

Concise Quintagrams®

33

1 Tied tennis score (5)

_ _ _ _ _

2 Protect (5)

_ _ _ _ _

3 Formal serving tray (6)

_ _ _ _ _ _

4 Pope (7)

_ _ _ _ _ _ _

5 Krakatoa's country (9)

_ _ _ _ _ _ _ _ _

A	A	A	C	D	D	D	E
E	E	E	F	F	G	I	I
I	L	N	N	N	O	O	P
R	R	S	S	T	U	U	V

34

1 Prohibit (3)

_ _ _

2 Slow-moving marsupial (5)

_ _ _ _ _

3 Succinct, brief (7)

_ _ _ _ _ _ _

4 Yellow powdery spice (8)

_ _ _ _ _ _ _ _

5 Savagely violent (9)

_ _ _ _ _ _ _ _ _

A	A	A	B	C	C	C	C
E	E	E	F	I	I	I	K
L	M	N	N	O	O	O	O
R	R	R	S	S	T	U	U

Concise Quintagrams®

35

1 Sombrero or homburg, eg (3)

_ _ _

2 Plant used to make linen (4)

_ _ _ _

3 Astrological diagram (6)

_ _ _ _ _ _

4 Caribbean percussion group (5,4)

_ _ _ _ _ _ _ _ _

5 British computing pioneer (4,6)

_ _ _ _ _ _ _ _ _ _

A	A	A	A	A	A	B	C
D	D	E	E	F	G	H	I
I	L	L	L	N	N	N	O
R	S	T	T	T	U	X	Z

36

1 Golfer's target score (3)

_ _ _

2 Elegance (5)

_ _ _ _ _

3 Branch of science (7)

_ _ _ _ _ _ _

4 Highly toxic toadstool (5,3)

_ _ _ _ _ _ _ _

5 Amass, hoard (9)

_ _ _ _ _ _ _ _ _

A	A	A	A	C	C	C	C
D	E	E	E	G	H	H	I
I	K	L	O	P	P	P	P
R	R	S	S	S	T	T	Y

Concise Quintagrams®

37

1 June 6, 1944 (1-3)

_ _ _

2 Gently remind (5)

_ _ _ _ _

3 Beaver's den (5)

_ _ _ _ _

4 Ship on display in Greenwich (5,4)

_ _ _ _ _ _ _ _ _

5 Dodgem (6,3)

_ _ _ _ _ _ _ _ _

A	A	A	B	C	C	D	D
D	D	E	E	E	G	G	K
L	M	N	O	P	R	R	R
S	T	T	U	U	U	Y	Y

38

1 Light-coloured (4)

_ _ _ _

2 Sales booth (5)

_ _ _ _ _

3 Ship's kitchen (6)

_ _ _ _ _ _

4 Short snappy joke (3-5)

_ _ _ _ _ _ _ _

5 Alert, attentive (2,3,4)

_ _ _ _ _ _ _ _ _

A	A	A	B	E	E	E	E
E	G	H	I	I	K	K	L
L	L	L	L	L	N	N	N
O	O	O	P	R	S	T	Y

Concise Quintagrams®

39

1 Interval, hiatus (3)

_ _ _

2 Pupil's wise adviser (6)

_ _ _ _ _ _

3 Ecclesiastical district (6)

_ _ _ _ _ _

4 Requiring gentle handling (8)

_ _ _ _ _ _ _ _

5 Dutch artist (9)

_ _ _ _ _ _ _ _ _

A	A	A	A	B	C	D	D
E	E	E	E	G	H	I	I
L	M	M	N	N	O	P	P
R	R	R	R	S	T	T	T

40

1 Whitewater boat (5)

_ _ _ _ _

2 Frank Sinatra standard (2,3)

_ _ _ _ _

3 Break into many pieces (7)

_ _ _ _ _ _ _

4 Imaginary mischief maker (7)

_ _ _ _ _ _ _

5 Positive thinking (8)

_ _ _ _ _ _ _ _

A	A	A	A	E	E	G	H
I	I	K	K	L	M	M
M	M	N	O	P	R	R	S
S	T	T	T	W	Y	Y	Y

Concise Quintagrams®

181

41

1 People (4)

_ _ _ _

2 Get hold of, understand (5)

_ _ _ _ _

3 Dangerous object or situation (6)

_ _ _ _ _ _

4 Small fruit containing a stone (7)

_ _ _ _ _ _ _

5 County town of Essex (10)

_ _ _ _ _ _ _ _ _ _

A	A	A	A	C	C	D	D
E	F	F	G	H	H	I	K
L	L	M	O	O	O	P	P
R	R	R	R	S	S	T	Z

42

1 Strongbox (4)

_ _ _ _

2 Undercover agent (4)

_ _ _ _

3 Jubilant (6)

_ _ _ _ _ _

4 Provide with water (8)

_ _ _ _ _ _ _ _

5 Former US president (6,4)

_ _ _ _ _ _ _ _ _ _

A	A	A	D	D	E	E	E
E	F	F	F	G	G	I	I
J	L	L	L	M	O	O	O
R	R	R	R	S	T	U	Y

Concise Quintagrams®

182

43

1 Open to debate (4)

_ _ _ _

2 Barbarian (5)

_ _ _ _ _

3 Baffling self-contradiction (7)

_ _ _ _ _ _ _

4 Needle-shaped monument (7)

_ _ _ _ _ _ _

5 Noisy disturbance (9)

_ _ _ _ _ _ _ _ _

A	A	B	B	C	D	E	E
I	I	K	L	M	M	M	N
O	O	O	O	O	O	O	P
R	R	S	T	T	T	U	X

44

1 Large stringed instrument (4)

_ _ _ _

2 Perform very well (5)

_ _ _ _ _

3 Hard rock used in construction (7)

_ _ _ _ _ _ _

4 Snail, oyster or octopus, eg (7)

_ _ _ _ _ _ _

5 Band that recorded *The Wall* (4,5)

_ _ _ _ _ _ _ _ _

A	A	C	C	D	E	E	E
F	G	H	I	I	K	L	L
L	L	M	N	N	O	O	P
P	R	R	S	T	U	X	Y

Concise Quintagrams®

183

45

1 Illegal activity (5)

_ _ _ _ _

2 Natural ability or style (5)

_ _ _ _ _

3 Wine often taken as an apéritif (6)

_ _ _ _ _ _

4 Satisfy (one's thirst) (6)

_ _ _ _ _ _

5 Highly social (10)

_ _ _ _ _ _ _ _ _ _

A	A	C	C	E	E	E	E
F	G	G	H	H	I	I	I
L	M	N	O	Q	R	R	R
R	R	R	S	S	U	U	Y

46

1 Piece of advice (3)

_ _ _

2 Lack of impartiality (4)

_ _ _ _

3 Study of the Earth's structure (7)

_ _ _ _ _ _ _

4 Normal, unexceptional (8)

_ _ _ _ _ _ _ _

5 Commonwealth nation (3,7)

_ _ _ _ _ _ _ _ _ _

A	A	A	A	B	D	D	E
E	E	G	G	I	I	I	L
L	N	N	N	O	O	O	P
R	R	S	T	W	Y	Y	Z

Concise Quintagrams®

47

1 Bard (4)

_ _ _ _

2 Very serious (5)

_ _ _ _ _

3 Puzzling question (6)

_ _ _ _ _ _

4 Spring flower (8)

_ _ _ _ _ _ _ _

5 Controversial subject (3,6)

_ _ _ _ _ _ _ _ _

A	A	B	B	D	D	E	E
E	E	E	G	H	I	L	L
L	L	O	O	O	O	P	P
R	R	T	T	T	U	V

48

1 Desire desperately (5)

_ _ _ _ _

2 Float along with the current (5)

_ _ _ _ _

3 Colourfully billed seabird (6)

_ _ _ _ _ _

4 Cleanliness (7)

_ _ _ _ _ _ _

5 Capital city of Somalia (9)

_ _ _ _ _ _ _ _ _

A	A	C	D	D	E	E	E
F	F	F	G	G	H	H	I
I	I	I	M	N	N	O	P
R	R	S	T	U	U	V	Y

Concise Quintagrams®

49

1 Froth (4)

_ _ _ _

2 Front part of a gun barrel (6)

_ _ _ _ _ _

3 Row of shops (6)

_ _ _ _ _ _

4 Japanese warrior (7)

_ _ _ _ _ _ _

5 Fill again (9)

_ _ _ _ _ _ _ _ _

A	A	A	A	A	D	E	E
E	E	F	H	I	I	L	L
M	M	M	N	O	P	P	R
R	R	S	S	U	U	Z	Z

50

1 Repair (4)

_ _ _ _

2 Dance performed in single file (5)

_ _ _ _ _

3 Hang pendulously (6)

_ _ _ _ _ _

4 Chemist's dispensary (8)

_ _ _ _ _ _ _ _

5 Tourist (9)

_ _ _ _ _ _ _ _ _

A	A	A	A	C	C	D	D
E	E	E	E	G	G	G	H
H	I	L	M	M	N	N	N
O	P	R	R	S	S	T	Y

Concise Quintagrams®

51

1 Crafty (3)

_ _ _

2 In plain view (5)

_ _ _ _ _

3 Welsh city (7)

_ _ _ _ _ _ _

4 Payment request (7)

_ _ _ _ _ _ _

5 Influential soul singer (6,4)

_ _ _ _ _ _ _ _ _ _

A	A	A	A	C	E	E	E
E	G	I	I	I	L	M	N
N	N	O	O	R	R	S	S
S	T	V	V	V	W	Y	Y

52

1 Bottle stopper (4)

_ _ _ _

2 Distinctive constellation (5)

_ _ _ _ _

3 Metal tool (7)

_ _ _ _ _ _ _

4 Attack with sustained shellfire (7)

_ _ _ _ _ _ _

5 Soft fruit (9)

_ _ _ _ _ _ _ _ _

A	A	A	B	B	B	C	D
E	E	I	K	M	N	N	N
O	O	O	O	P	P	R	R
R	R	R	R	R	S	S	Y

Concise Quintagrams®

53

1 Playful enjoyment (3)

_ _ _

2 Pavement edge (4)

_ _ _ _

3 Voice box (6)

_ _ _ _ _ _

4 Supportive of one's country (9)

_ _ _ _ _ _ _ _ _

5 Dickens novel (5,5)

_ _ _ _ _ _ _ _ _ _

A	A	A	B	B	C	E	E
E	F	H	I	I	K	K	L
L	N	N	O	O	P	R	R
R	S	T	T	U	U	X	Y

54

1 Civic dignitary (5)

_ _ _ _ _

2 Velocity (5)

_ _ _ _ _

3 Rub to a shine (6)

_ _ _ _ _ _

4 Rock-pool mollusc (6)

_ _ _ _ _ _

5 Lindisfarne (4,6)

_ _ _ _ _ _ _ _ _ _

A	A	D	D	E	E	E	H
H	I	I	I	L	L	L	L
M	M	N	O	O	O	P	P
P	R	S	S	S	T	Y	Y

Concise Quintagrams®

55

1 Brief swim (3)

_ _ _

2 Upper part of a dress (6)

_ _ _ _ _ _

3 Impartial (7)

_ _ _ _ _ _ _

4 Special anniversary (7)

_ _ _ _ _ _ _

5 Currant biscuit (9)

_ _ _ _ _ _ _ _ _

A	A	A	B	B	B	C	D
D	D	E	E	E	E	G	I
I	I	I	I	J	L	L	L
N	O	P	R	R	T	U	U

56

1 Short hairstyle (3)

_ _ _

2 Nursery (6)

_ _ _ _ _ _

3 Athletics implement (6)

_ _ _ _ _ _

4 Ancient elephant-like mammal (8)

_ _ _ _ _ _ _ _

5 Superlatively beautiful (9)

_ _ _ _ _ _ _ _ _

A	B	B	C	C	C	D	D
E	E	E	E	H	I	I	I
M	N	O	O	O	Q	R	S
S	S	S	T	T	U	U	X

Concise Quintagrams®

57

1 Resign (4)

_ _ _ _

2 Hickory nut (5)

_ _ _ _ _

3 Uncontrolled mental state (6)

_ _ _ _ _ _

4 Leaves (7)

_ _ _ _ _ _ _

5 Creator of the Famous Five (4,6)

_ _ _ _ _ _ _ _ _ _

A	A	B	C	D	E	E	E
E	F	F	G	I	I	I	L
L	N	N	N	O	O	P
Q	R	T	T	U	Y	Y	Z

58

1 Beehive product (5)

_ _ _ _ _

2 Legendary cursed king (5)

_ _ _ _ _

3 Warm hooded anorak (5)

_ _ _ _ _

4 Free from captivity (8)

_ _ _ _ _ _ _ _

5 Attractive garden bird (9)

_ _ _ _ _ _ _ _ _

A	A	A	A	B	C	D	D
E	E	E	F	G	H	H	I
I	I	K	L	L	M	N	N
O	O	P	R	R	S	T	Y

59

1 Gesture of agreement (3)

_ _ _

2 Highly conductive metal (6)

_ _ _ _ _ _

3 Gambling card game (7)

_ _ _ _ _ _ _

4 African desert (8)

_ _ _ _ _ _ _ _

5 Individually (3,2,3)

_ _ _ _ _ _ _ _

A	A	A	B	C	D	E	E
E	H	I	K	L	N	N	N
N	N	O	O	O	O	O	O
O	P	P	P	R	R	T	Y

60

1 Garden water feature (4)

_ _ _ _

2 Strike with an open palm (4)

_ _ _ _

3 Unsteady infant (7)

_ _ _ _ _ _ _

4 Naval vessel (7)

_ _ _ _ _ _ _

5 Lake poet (10)

_ _ _ _ _ _ _ _ _ _

A	A	D	D	D	D	E	E
F	G	H	I	L	L	N	O
O	O	O	P	P	R	R	R
R	S	S	T	T	T	W	W

Concise Quintagrams®

61

1 Martial art (4)

_ _ _ _

2 Parody (5)

_ _ _ _ _

3 Orator's platform (7)

_ _ _ _ _ _ _

4 Colourful public celebration (7)

_ _ _ _ _ _ _

5 Translate, make intelligible (9)

_ _ _ _ _ _ _ _ _

A	A	D	E	E	E	F	G
I	J	M	N	N	O	O	O
O	P	P	P	R	R	R	R
S	S	T	T	T	T	U	U

62

1 Midday (4)

_ _ _ _

2 Quick-witted, keen of mind (5)

_ _ _ _ _

3 Negotiate a price (6)

_ _ _ _ _ _

4 Elementary particle (8)

_ _ _ _ _ _ _ _

5 Ancient Egyptian queen (9)

_ _ _ _ _ _ _ _ _

A	A	A	A	C	C	E	E
E	E	G	G	H	H	L	L
L	N	N	N	O	O	O	O
P	P	R	R	R	S	T	T

Concise Quintagrams®

63

1 Bluebottle or gnat, eg (3)

_ _ _

2 Dazzling light (5)

_ _ _ _ _

3 Roman equivalent of Hermes (7)

_ _ _ _ _ _ _

4 Abstaining from alcohol (8)

_ _ _ _ _ _ _ _

5 Point of entry (9)

_ _ _ _ _ _ _ _ _

A	A	C	D	E	E	E	E
E	F	G	H	H	L	L	L
L	M	O	O	R	R	R	R
S	T	T	T	U	Y	Y	

64

1 Actor's prompt (3)

_ _ _

2 Play for time (5)

_ _ _ _ _

3 Chivalrous (7)

_ _ _ _ _ _ _

4 Danger, risk (8)

_ _ _ _ _ _ _ _

5 Juicy (9)

_ _ _ _ _ _ _ _ _

A	A	A	A	C	C	C	D
E	E	E	G	J	L	L	L
L	L	N	N	O	P	R	S
S	T	T	T	U	U	U	Y

Concise Quintagrams®

65

1 Just for show (4)

— — — —

2 Hunting trip in S Africa: a long way, I must conclude (6)

— — — — — —

3 Eurostar, if forced, displaying list of prices (6)

— — — — — —

4 Artist cheers loudly: one with a drink (7)

— — — — — — —

5 Disturbed tsarist is mocking writers (9)

— — — — — — — — —

A	A	A	A	A	A	A	A
F	F	F	F	F	I	I	I
I	I	I	R	R	R	R	R
S	S	S	S	T	T	T	T

66

1 Cautious fighting unknown quantity (4)

— — — —

2 Keen cooking joint (4)

— — — —

3 Clown and I make mistake filling receptacle (7)

— — — — — — —

4 London station: woman falls (8)

— — — — — — — —

5 Pick leader in secret ballot (9)

— — — — — — — — —

A	A	C	C	E	E	E	E
E	I	I	I	K	K	L	N
N	O	O	O	P	R	R	R
R	S	T	T	T	V	W	Y

Cryptic Quintagrams®

67

1 In retrospect, poet's lacklustre (4)

— — — —

2 Characters in burlesque always spill the beans (6)

— — — — — —

3 Gave the appearance of feeding bananas (7)

— — — — — — —

4 Queen returning home after mother and son stays put (7)

— — — — — — —

5 Declining area represented by Ulster councillor? (8)

— — — — — — — —

A	A	A	A	B	D	D	D
D	E	E	E	E	F	G	I
I	L	M	N	N	N	O	Q
R	R	R	S	S	U	W	W

68

1 Gather whiskey's left to mature (5)

— — — — —

2 Note sounding a bit deeper rose, perhaps (6)

— — — — — —

3 Choose the French relish (6)

— — — — — —

4 Barely in charge of European legal administration (7)

— — — — — — —

5 One's quit about problem (8)

— — — — — — — —

C	C	E	E	E	E	F	G
I	I	I	J	K	L	L	N
O	O	O	P	P	Q	R	R
S	S	T	T	U	U	U	W

Cryptic Quintagrams®

69

1 Rejected loan for vehicle (3)

_ _ _

2 Fool's mate taking pawn (5)

_ _ _ _ _

3 Snatch last of beer in bar (7)

_ _ _ _ _ _ _

4 Action outside called insane (8)

_ _ _ _ _ _ _ _

5 Cedar tree that can be cloned? (9)

_ _ _ _ _ _ _ _ _

A	A	B	C	C	C	D	D
D	E	E	E	E	E	E	E
G	H	M	N	P	P	R	R
R	R	S	T	T	U	U	X

70

1 Just beat one entering very quietly (3)

_ _ _

2 Activity centre maybe has chap going around four (4)

_ _ _ _

3 Staff given "royal" label (7)

_ _ _ _ _ _ _

4 The task, strangely, to get hold of new capital (8)

_ _ _ _ _ _ _ _

5 Melon from tin turned out pale (10)

_ _ _ _ _ _ _ _ _ _

A	A	A	C	C	E	E	E
E	H	H	I	I	I	K	K
L	N	N	O	P	P	P	R
S	S	T	T	T	U	V	

Cryptic Quintagrams®

71

1 Gentle like this newspaper (4)

_ _ _ _

2 Firm accepting communist set of beliefs (5)

_ _ _ _ _

3 A number try and hit shot (6)

_ _ _ _ _ _

4 Changing of the Guard for girl (8)

_ _ _ _ _ _ _ _

5 Party member, dependable and PC (9)

_ _ _ _ _ _ _ _ _

A	A	B	C	C	D	D	E
E	E	F	G	H	H	I	L
N	O	O	O	R	R	R	S
S	T	T	T	T	T	U	Y

72

1 Extract stone from mine (3)

_ _ _

2 Page in revised A to Z is a gem (5)

_ _ _ _ _

3 Damsels at heart are exhibiting gender bias (6)

_ _ _ _ _ _

4 Sue is in plain language charming (9)

_ _ _ _ _ _ _ _ _

5 Defectors from East get on? That's right (9)

_ _ _ _ _ _ _ _ _

A	A	A	B	C	D	E	E
E	I	I	O	O	O	P	P
P	R	R	R	S	S	S	S
T	T	T	T	T	U	X	Z

Cryptic Quintagrams®

73

1 Turner's lake, cutter going round (4)

_ _ _ _

2 Confusion you see in calendar, reportedly (4)

_ _ _ _

3 Last from disreputable joke stock (5)

_ _ _ _ _

4 Verdict Jung meted out (9)

_ _ _ _ _ _ _ _ _

5 Paid evening visitor whose charges are small? (10)

_ _ _ _ _ _ _ _ _ _

A	A	A	B	B	D	D	E
E	E	E	E	E	G	I	I
J	L	M	N	P	Q	R	S
T	T	T	U	U	X	Y	Z

74

1 Envious politician (5)

_ _ _ _ _

2 Appropriate ceremony in the auditorium? (5)

_ _ _ _ _

3 Type of betting odds to study (6)

_ _ _ _ _ _

4 Ruling party perfect, article admitted (8)

_ _ _ _ _ _ _ _

5 Writer of tales, say, is talented (8)

_ _ _ _ _ _ _ _

A	A	A	D	D	E	E	E
E	G	G	H	I	I	I	M
N	N	N	O	P	R	R	R
S	S	S	S	T	T	T	Y

Cryptic Quintagrams®

75

1 Dock workers organised in retirement (3)

— — —

2 Business vehicle (5)

— — — — —

3 Commotion when America follows behind (6)

— — — — — —

4 To flatter entertaining Conservative is a bloomer (9)

— — — — — — — — —

5 Snake trap's done for Russian novelist (9)

— — — — — — — — —

A	A	B	C	C	C	E	E
K	K	M	N	P	P	P	R
R	R	R	S	S	T	T	T
T	T	U	U	U	U	U	U

76

1 What's earned with maturity (4)

— — — —

2 Times policy shows where journalist's name is written (6)

— — — — — —

3 Mad Hatter's baleful remark (6)

— — — — — —

4 Knave with drug money won gambling (7)

— — — — — — —

5 Brilliance of sergeants doing manoeuvres (9)

— — — — — — — — —

A	A	A	A	B	C	E	E
E	E	E	G	G	H	I	J
K	L	N	N	O	P	R	R
S	S	T	T	T	T	W	Y

Cryptic Quintagrams®

77

1 Good people in favour (5)

_ _ _ _ _

2 Street with place for taxi to wait (5)

_ _ _ _ _

3 Seabird getting home on a short burst of wind (6)

_ _ _ _ _ _

4 Queen on board ship shows long narrow flag (8)

_ _ _ _ _ _ _ _

5 Man going after source of grapes that's sour (8)

_ _ _ _ _ _ _ _

A	A	A	A	C	D	E	E
E	E	F	F	G	G	I	I
M	N	N	N	P	R	R	R
R	S	S	T	T	U	V	Y

78

1 Song from that man on the radio (4)

_ _ _ _

2 Unusual getting second chances (4)

_ _ _ _

3 Letter from Kuwait, chatty (5)

_ _ _ _

4 Built with care, redeveloped to minimise friction (9)

_ _ _ _ _ _ _ _ _

5 Constant lack of practice causes irritability (10)

_ _ _ _ _ _ _ _ _ _

A	A	B	C	C	C	D	D
E	E	H	H	I	I	I	L
M	N	N	O	R	R	S	S
S	S	T	T	T	U	U	Y

Cryptic Quintagrams®

79

1 Still one creature of great height! (4)

_ _ _ _

2 Miser generally keeps stuff (5)

_ _ _ _ _

3 Painter has redness regularly after massage (6)

_ _ _ _ _ _

4 By which meatballs are made from stale lamb? (7)

_ _ _ _ _ _ _

5 Grounds fit for fair (10)

_ _ _ _ _ _ _ _ _ _

A	A	A	A	A	B	B	E
E	E	E	E	E	G	G	I
L	M	N	N	N	O	R	R
R	R	S	S	S	T	U	Y

80

1 Ordered wicked stimulant (4)

_ _ _ _

2 Seductress picked up furs (4)

_ _ _ _

3 Politician's high treason (7)

_ _ _ _ _ _ _

4 Modern musician backing wife's cover (7)

_ _ _ _ _ _ _

5 Charlatan to launch online investment platform? (10)

_ _ _ _ _ _ _ _ _ _

A	A	A	A	B	B	D	E
E	E	E	I	K	M	M	N
N	N	N	O	O	P	P	R
R	R	S	T	T	U	W	X

Cryptic Quintagrams®

81

1 Leave completely, shunning the European (4)

_ _ _ _

2 Thatcher's first to abolish society burdens (5)

_ _ _ _ _

3 Chap who's not long home? (6)

_ _ _ _ _ _

4 Took a fall — stomach was bleeding (7)

_ _ _ _ _ _ _

5 Small amount of sulphur being important (10)

_ _ _ _ _ _ _ _ _ _

A	A	B	D	E	E	E	G
I	I	I	J	L	M	M	N
N	Q	R	S	S	S	T	T
T	T	T	T	U	U	U	X

82

1 Mild oath regularly used in England (4)

_ _ _ _

2 Vehicle, one on test (4)

_ _ _ _

3 Machine shaping articles from either side of the Channel (5)

_ _ _ _ _

4 Bar supporting clerk (9)

_ _ _ _ _ _ _ _ _

5 Cheap title rewritten with instinctive feeling (10)

_ _ _ _ _ _ _ _ _ _

A	A	A	A	B	C	C	D
E	E	E	E	E	G	H	H
I	I	I	L	L	O	P	P
R	R	S	T	T	T	T	X

Cryptic Quintagrams®

83

1 Put on commercial broadcast (3)

— — —

2 Bright twin girls heading for doctorates (5)

— — — — —

3 Swear nothing must get in the way (6)

— — — — — —

4 Over-optimistic and endlessly speedy, penning nine books (8)

— — — — — — — —

5 Problem with lift right for someone looking for one (10)

— — — — — — — — — —

A	C	C	C	D	D	D	E
E	H	H	H	I	I	I	I
I	I	K	O	O	Q	R	R
S	T	T	U	U	V	V	X

84

1 Husband with assistance (4)

— — — —

2 The best in Chinese literature (5)

— — — — —

3 Bar opposite (7)

— — — — — — —

4 The greatest drink? Mere bubbly! (7)

— — — — — — —

5 Focus attention on snub involving trophy (9)

— — — — — — — — —

A	C	D	E	E	E	E	E
G	H	H	I	I	L	L	M
N	N	O	O	P	P	R	R
S	S	T	T	T	T	U	U

Cryptic Quintagrams®

85

1 Protection from father given to daughter (3)

— — —

2 Cosmetic drug to put in container (5)

— — — — —

3 Priest sporting mark on uniform (6)

— — — — — —

4 Very laconic, rarely liable to erupt (8)

— — — — — — — —

5 Pronouncement of guilt that's firmly believed in (10)

— — — — — — — — — —

A	A	B	C	C	C	C	D
E	I	I	I	I	L	N	N
N	O	O	O	O	O	P	P
R	S	T	T	T	V	V	X

86

1 Hide from shower (4)

— — — —

2 Antelope seen in English countryside (5)

— — — — —

3 One doing badly is blue (6)

— — — — — —

4 Magician putting sulphur in correct hole (8)

— — — — — — — —

5 Dramatic exit for men ruined rodeo (5,4)

— — — — — — — — —

A	A	D	D	D	E	E	E
E	G	G	I	I	L	L	N
N	O	O	O	O	O	P	P
P	R	R	R	S	S	T	T

Cryptic Quintagrams®

87

1 Tradesman's couple of family members (5)

_ _ _ _ _

2 Complain alcohol's swallowed hot (5)

_ _ _ _ _

3 Providers of material in German novel (6)

_ _ _ _ _ _

4 Leave a portion of kebab and onion (7)

_ _ _ _ _ _ _

5 Lose one's temper with penniless financial firm (9)

_ _ _ _ _ _ _ _ _

A	A	A	A	A	B	B	D
E	E	E	E	G	G	H	I
K	M	M	N	N	N	N	N
O	O	O	R	R	R	S	W

88

1 Millions request means of achieving anonymity (4)

_ _ _ _

2 Manage to find time to compete at athletics? (5)

_ _ _ _ _

3 One certain to follow the French in liberty (7)

_ _ _ _ _ _ _

4 Alarm, just surrounded by marsh (8)

_ _ _ _ _ _ _ _

5 Formal garden section nearly went wrong (8)

_ _ _ _ _ _ _ _

A	A	A	C	E	E	E	E
E	E	F	G	H	I	I	K
L	M	N	P	R	R	R	R
R	R	S	S	T	T	T	U

Cryptic Quintagrams®

89

1 Carnivore's stomach (4)

_ _ _ _

2 Coppers find writer attending church (5)

_ _ _ _ _

3 Tudor garment Bottom uses, but not Snout (7)

_ _ _ _ _ _ _

4 Lively curses about publicity campaigns (8)

_ _ _ _ _ _ _ _

5 Top drivers should, if flagged down (8)

_ _ _ _ _ _ _ _

A	A	B	B	C	C	D	D
E	E	E	E	E	E	L	L
L	N	O	O	P	P	R	R
R	S	S	T	U	U	U	V

90

1 Party good to follow (3)

_ _ _

2 Painter unknown in Indian state (4)

_ _ _ _

3 Who might appear now light dissipates? (5,3)

_ _ _ _ _ _ _ _

4 Stable with one acceptable horse (8)

_ _ _ _ _ _ _ _

5 Killing mirth on Sunday primarily (9)

_ _ _ _ _ _ _ _ _

A	A	A	D	E	G	G	G
G	H	H	I	I	L	L	L
L	N	N	O	O	O	O	R
S	S	T	T	T	U	W	Y

Cryptic Quintagrams®

91

1 Long-distance runner from Kiel inexplicably keeled over (4)

_ _ _ _

2 Work out form (6)

_ _ _ _ _ _

3 Celebrity on edge (6)

_ _ _ _ _ _

4 Regular honey drink certain to be taken inside (8)

_ _ _ _ _ _ _ _

5 Form of allowance Olympian squandered (8)

_ _ _ _ _ _ _ _

A	A	D	D	E	E	E	E
E	E	F	G	G	I	I	I
L	L	L	M	M	N	N	N
O	P	R	R	S	U	U	Y

92

1 Wife remains clean (4)

_ _ _ _

2 Liberal president once kind (4)

_ _ _ _

3 TS Eliot works showing rhetorical effect (7)

_ _ _ _ _ _ _

4 Uphold smear about crossworders (7)

_ _ _ _ _ _ _

5 Get in wild gathering completely (10)

_ _ _ _ _ _ _ _ _ _

A	A	A	E	E	E	G	H
I	I	I	I	K	L	L	L
L	N	N	O	R	S	S	S
S	T	T	T	T	U	W	Y

Cryptic Quintagrams®

93

1 Walk stiffly with support (5)

— — — — —

2 Confidence trick really upset some takers at first (5)

— — — — —

3 Fatal delay, confused about day (6)

— — — — — —

4 Passionate plot of novel about male (6)

— — — — — —

5 Military style of walking races. They're mad! (5,5)

— — — — — — — — — —

A	A	A	C	D	D	E	E
H	H	L	M	M	O	R	R
R	R	R	S	S	S	S	T
T	T	T	U	U	Y	Y

94

1 Top mimic given a kiss (4)

— — — —

2 Crooner embracing Italian tart (6)

— — — — — —

3 English men mentioned in dispatches? (6)

— — — — — —

4 What may be left from extremely brave expedition (7)

— — — — — — —

5 Diffusion's less rapid at sea (9)

— — — — — — — — —

A	A	A	B	B	D	E	E
E	E	E	G	I	I	I	I
L	L	M	N	P	P	Q	R
S	S	S	S	T	T	U	X

Cryptic Quintagrams®

95

1 Real purse you'd pick up (5)

_ _ _ _ _

2 Canadian territory that surrounds this country (5)

_ _ _ _ _

3 Watch in room, wound, keeping time (7)

_ _ _ _ _ _ _

4 Last Letter from America, about historian and apostles' father (7)

_ _ _ _ _ _ _

5 Soldier dropped and left loose change in place, apparently (8)

_ _ _ _ _ _ _ _

A	A	A	A	B	D	E	E
E	E	I	K	K	K	L	L
M	N	N	O	O	O	P	P
R	R	T	U	U	X	Y	Z

96

1 Twist piece of silk in knots (4)

_ _ _ _

2 Proposal after beginning to caress chest (6)

_ _ _ _ _ _

3 Working parties move reluctantly (7)

_ _ _ _ _ _ _

4 Time to go on platform for opinions (7)

_ _ _ _ _ _ _

5 Fish sink crossing lake (8)

_ _ _ _ _ _ _ _

A	C	D	E	E	E	E	F
F	F	I	I	I	K	K	L
N	N	O	O	P	R	R	R
R	S	T	T	T	T	U	W

97

1 Family left in American gaol (4)

_ _ _ _

2 Vegetable used in Christmas pudding (4)

_ _ _ _

3 Country affording admission for Ms Jong? (7)

_ _ _ _ _ _ _

4 Pinta? There's little energy in some pints (7)

_ _ _ _ _ _ _

5 Begin a Zola novel? It's thick and rich in character (10)

_ _ _ _ _ _ _ _ _ _

A	A	A	A	A	A	B	C
C	D	E	E	E	G	G	I
I	L	L	L	L	M	N	N
N	O	O	P	R	S	U	Z

98

1 Reportedly compelled as a domestic servant (4)

_ _ _ _

2 The end is nigh (5)

_ _ _ _ _

3 Feasts abroad, most free from risk (6)

_ _ _ _ _ _

4 Rubbish written about decline in beauty contests (8)

_ _ _ _ _ _ _ _

5 Standard teachers, perhaps, in Arizona city (9)

_ _ _ _ _ _ _ _ _

A	A	A	A	A	A	C	D
E	E	E	F	F	F	F	G
G	I	L	L	M	N	O	P
S	S	S	S	S	T	T	T

Cryptic Quintagrams®

99

1 Sunday roast shared? (5)

_ _ _ _ _

2 Train regularly carrying former character from Dallas? (5)

_ _ _ _ _

3 Tabloid published French recipe (6)

_ _ _ _ _ _

4 Spoken of conifer and pine in the distance (7)

_ _ _ _ _ _ _

5 Mysterious Green Lady of myth (9)

_ _ _ _ _ _ _ _ _

A	A	A	D	E	E	E	F
G	G	G	I	J	L	L	N
N	N	N	O	O	O	R	R
R	T	T	T	U	U	X	Y

100

1 Minister's heading off crime (5)

_ _ _ _ _

2 Revel in audition's distinctive language (6)

_ _ _ _ _ _

3 Spaniard maybe to keep twisting lieutenant's elbow (6)

_ _ _ _ _ _

4 Salesman and I press union to back plant (7)

_ _ _ _ _ _ _

5 Hail arak distilled in desert (8)

_ _ _ _ _ _ _ _

A	A	A	A	A	B	E	E
E	H	I	I	J	J	K	L
L	N	N	O	O	P	Q	R
R	R	S	S	S	T	U	U

Cryptic Quintagrams®

101

1 Toy dog — or boxer (3)

— — —

2 Returning to the old part of Chiswick (4)

— — — —

3 Street song that may lift one? (5)

— — — — —

4 Proposed position for part of hospital (3,7)

— — — — — — — — — —

5 Diet of Worms? (10)

— — — — — — — — — —

A	A	C	D	E	E	E	F
G	I	I	I	L	L	M	O
O	P	P	R	R	R	R	S
T	T	T	U	U	V	W	Y

102

1 Decline small sweet (4)

— — — —

2 Keen to press old skirt (5)

— — — — —

3 Check famous dictionary for "prohibited" (6)

— — — — — —

4 Quantity of paper concealing vagrant's large bottle (8)

— — — — — — — —

5 Meats cooked in table wine will (9)

— — — — — — — — —

A	A	A	B	D	D	D	E
E	E	E	E	H	I	M	M
N	O	O	O	O	O	P	R
R	S	T	T	T	T	V	V

Cryptic Quintagrams®

103

1 Go around old city of legend (4)

_ _ _ _

2 Monster to get canonised? (5)

_ _ _ _ _

3 Out to lunch, eating a stew (6)

_ _ _ _ _ _

4 African port with a more piquant flavour (7)

_ _ _ _ _ _ _

5 Fan of united states dined with queen and celebrities (10)

_ _ _ _ _ _ _ _ _ _

A	A	A	A	B	D	E	E
E	E	E	F	G	G	I	I
I	L	N	N	O	R	R	R
S	S	T	T	T	T	T	Y

104

1 Unlucky Jill has lost Jack (3)

_ _ _

2 Go without European peace (5)

_ _ _ _ _

3 Claimed free check-up (7)

_ _ _ _ _ _ _

4 I'm given whiter sticker (7)

_ _ _ _ _ _ _

5 Food sloppy setter's taken for hack work? (4,6)

_ _ _ _ _ _ _ _ _ _

A	A	B	C	D	E	E	E
E	E	G	I	I	I	I	L
L	L	L	M	M	P	Q	R
R	R	S	T	T	T	U	U

Cryptic Quintagrams®

105

1 No amateur occupies an extended part of stage (5)

_ _ _ _ _

2 Disparate cast, or its members? (6)

_ _ _ _ _ _

3 Best teacher's last textbook (6)

_ _ _ _ _ _

4 Where letters may be left after fight (7)

_ _ _ _ _ _ _

5 What's inside provides satisfaction (8)

_ _ _ _ _ _ _ _

A	A	B	C	C	E	E	I
M	N	N	N	O	O	O	O
O	P	P	P	R	R	R	R
S	S	S	T	T	T	T	X

106

1 Wrestling ring needs amount of money up front (4)

_ _ _ _

2 Stick kept around home for dog (6)

_ _ _ _ _ _

3 One's left home before catching Russian plane (6)

_ _ _ _ _ _

4 Imagine what you might do if sleepwalking (5,2)

_ _ _ _ _ _ _

5 Starter I finished in Nato mess? (9)

_ _ _ _ _ _ _ _ _

A	A	A	A	C	D	E	E
E	E	G	I	I	I	M	M
M	N	N	N	O	O	P	P
R	R	S	S	T	T	U	U

Cryptic Quintagrams®

214

107

1 Compulsory payment regressive at times (3)

_ _ _

2 Hardly fair or fitting (4)

_ _ _ _

3 Devious guards aren't virtuous (7)

_ _ _ _ _ _ _

4 Most careful teacher is sadly short of energy (8)

_ _ _ _ _ _ _ _

5 Castigate faithful supporter hiding at home (10)

_ _ _ _ _ _ _ _ _ _

A	A	A	C	C	D	E	E
H	I	I	I	I	I	J	L
L	N	N	P	R	S	S	S
S	T	T	T	T	U	X	Y

108

1 Run after chap for fruit (5)

_ _ _ _ _

2 A person generally is attached to Australian sea air (5)

_ _ _ _ _

3 Go over fault (6)

_ _ _ _ _ _

4 Portuguese, perhaps, at home entertaining police chief (7)

_ _ _ _ _ _ _

5 Covering the foot pedal and knee when cycling? (5-4)

_ _ _ _ _ _ _ _ _

A	A	A	B	C	D	D	E
E	E	E	E	E	E	F	G
I	I	K	L	M	N	N	N
N	O	O	O	P	R	T	Z

Cryptic Quintagrams®

109

1 Better EU policy (3)

_ _ _

2 Line from letter read out (5)

_ _ _ _ _

3 Prison for men almost completely enclosed (6)

_ _ _ _ _ _

4 Oxidation on film causing suspicion (8)

_ _ _ _ _ _ _ _

5 Nappy later changed, by the look of it (10)

_ _ _ _ _ _ _ _ _ _

A	A	A	A	A	C	E	E
E	G	I	L	L	M	N	P
P	P	Q	R	R	S	S	S
T	T	T	U	U	U	Y	

110

1 Scope — ace doctor needs it (5)

_ _ _ _ _

2 Initially advise duke about campaign medal (5)

_ _ _ _ _

3 This directs players to stay at wicket (5)

_ _ _ _ _

4 Father's fur is fair (8)

_ _ _ _ _ _ _ _

5 Derelict flats suit musicians (9)

_ _ _ _ _ _ _ _ _

A	A	A	A	A	A	A	B
B	B	D	E	F	I	I	L
L	M	N	O	P	R	S	S
S	S	T	T	T	T	U	W

Cryptic Quintagrams®

111

1 Naturally gifted in job, or not (4)

_ _ _ _

2 Rarely paid stooge (4)

_ _ _ _

3 Hue and cry over with (6)

_ _ _ _ _ _

4 Science subject: like essay describing new moon (9)

_ _ _ _ _ _ _ _ _

5 Shot after defender's rebounded (9)

_ _ _ _ _ _ _ _ _

A	A	B	B	C	D	D	E
E	E	E	F	F	I	K	L
L	M	N	N	O	O	O	O
R	R	R	S	T	W	Y	Y

112

1 Asian prince somewhat open to return (4)

_ _ _ _

2 Provide crack for internet users? (5)

_ _ _ _ _

3 Singular paper for gentleman (6)

_ _ _ _ _ _

4 Following drink, actors will be miserable (8)

_ _ _ _ _ _ _ _

5 Depiction of some sunlight going through doorway (9)

_ _ _ _ _ _ _ _ _

A	A	A	A	A	C	D	E
E	I	I	J	L	N	O	O
P	P	Q	Q	R	R	R	R
S	S	T	T	U	U	W	Y

Cryptic Quintagrams®

113

1 Foreign currency: fortune in unknown amounts (5)

_ _ _ _ _

2 Ace is being listened to in hospital room (6)

_ _ _ _ _ _

3 Instrument in Ritz he played (6)

_ _ _ _ _ _

4 Buzzer rounds transformed quiz game (7)

_ _ _ _ _ _ _

5 Very small rival to fight (8)

_ _ _ _ _ _ _ _

A	A	B	B	C	D	E	E
E	H	H	I	I	I	L	M
O	O	Q	R	R	T	T	T
U	W	X	Y	Z	Z	Z	Z

114

1 Behind, in arrears (4)

_ _ _ _

2 A lot may go here working round university (7)

_ _ _ _ _ _ _

3 First hole (7)

_ _ _ _ _ _ _

4 Relaxing, fluster having been resolved (7)

_ _ _ _ _ _ _

5 FBI agents in set piece (7)

_ _ _ _ _ _ _

A	A	C	E	E	E	E	E
F	G	G	I	I	L	M	N
N	N	N	O	O	P	R	R
R	S	S	T	T	T	U	U

Cryptic Quintagrams®

115

1 Talking bird (4)

_ _ _ _

2 Firm embracing revolutionary beliefs (5)

_ _ _ _ _

3 Former African National Park (6)

_ _ _ _ _ _

4 Troops ordered to hide equipment (7)

_ _ _ _ _ _ _

5 Represented ritual as an orgy (10)

_ _ _ _ _ _ _ _ _ _

A	A	A	A	A	B	C	C
D	D	E	E	E	G	H	I
I	L	M	N	O	O	O	R
R	R	R	S	T	T	U	X

116

1 Work with aluminium and stone (4)

_ _ _ _

2 Tree in quiet rural road (5)

_ _ _ _ _

3 Chess tactic? The most important one (7)

_ _ _ _ _ _ _

4 Reorganisation of SkyTech Limited? (7)

_ _ _ _ _ _ _

5 Old mercenary gets shelter over in foreign country? (9)

_ _ _ _ _ _ _ _ _

A	A	A	C	C	E	E	E
E	E	F	G	H	I	I	K
K	L	L	L	N	N	N	N
O	P	P	P	R	S	T	Y

Cryptic Quintagrams®

117

1 Decayed organ producing gas (5)

_ _ _ _ _

2 Quail and songbird crossing lake (6)

_ _ _ _ _ _

3 Expert able to make money (6)

_ _ _ _ _ _

4 Greens in lower house (7)

_ _ _ _ _ _ _

5 Doctor admitting possible cause of death (8)

_ _ _ _ _ _ _ _

A	C	C	D	F	F	G	G
H	I	I	I	L	M	M	N
N	N	N	N	O	O	O	O
O	P	R	R	R	S	T	W

118

1 Buzzer or series of buttons? (3)

_ _ _

2 Hard: a radio presenter's religious journey (4)

_ _ _ _

3 Home often having tower in front of it? (7)

_ _ _ _ _ _ _

4 Play small person briefly next to a celebrity (9)

_ _ _ _ _ _ _ _ _

5 Something to sharpen teeth's now deployed (9)

_ _ _ _ _ _ _ _ _

A	A	A	A	A	C	D	E
E	F	G	H	H	I	J	L
L	M	N	N	N	O	O	P
R	S	T	T	V	W	Y	Y

Cryptic Quintagrams®

119

1 Don't stop being an idiot (4)

— — — —

2 Satyr plays deviate from moral standards (5)

— — — — —

3 A number perform meditative discipline (5)

— — — — —

4 Lines functioning as Latin exercise (8)

— — — — — — — —

5 Poor kid rejected jelly and cake (10)

— — — — — — — — — —

A	A	A	A	A	D	E	F
F	G	G	I	I	M	N	N
N	N	O	O	O	Q	R	R
R	S	T	T	U	U	Y	Z

120

1 Commander edges away from infidel (3)

— — —

2 Towards one side as garden suburb (5)

— — — — —

3 Defeat heavily in field event (6)

— — — — — —

4 Space travelling is Mike's fantasy (8)

— — — — — — — —

5 There's very little help for timekeeper (6,4)

— — — — — — — — — —

A	A	A	A	A	A	C	D
E	E	E	E	G	H	H	I
I	K	M	M	M	M	N	N
P	R	S	S	S	T	U	W

Cryptic Quintagrams®

121

1 Have taped king today (4)

_ _ _ _

2 Artist left after nothing said (4)

_ _ _ _

3 Original story (5)

_ _ _ _ _

4 Put out in prelim, in a tent (9)

_ _ _ _ _ _ _ _ _

5 Chances of advancement, taking in university brochure (10)

_ _ _ _ _ _ _ _ _ _

A	A	C	E	E	E	E	I
I	K	L	L	L	M	N	N
N	O	O	O	O	P	P	R
R	S	S	T	T	U	V	W

122

1 Tree trunk? (3)

_ _ _

2 Unadorned stone vessel (5)

_ _ _ _ _

3 How sad, stray dog (6)

_ _ _ _ _ _

4 Seizes £1,000,000? (8)

_ _ _ _ _ _ _ _

5 Slightly spoil drink with friend (10)

_ _ _ _ _ _ _ _ _ _

A	A	A	A	B	D	D	G
H	I	I	K	L	L	M	M
N	N	O	O	O	P	R	R
S	S	S	T	U	W	X	Y

Cryptic Quintagrams®

123

1 Posh vehicle returning within two miles (4)

_ _ _ _

2 Rev vehicle when following girl (5)

_ _ _ _ _

3 Fashionable, having several channels? (6)

_ _ _ _ _ _

4 Within month, finally you risk getting illness (8)

_ _ _ _ _ _ _ _

5 Sex up dead moves for dance (3,2,4)

_ _ _ _ _ _ _ _ _

A	A	A	C	C	D	D	D
E	E	E	G	I	I	I	J
L	M	N	O	O	O	P	R
R	S	U	U	V	V	X	Y

124

1 Extremes of harmony musician used for vocal work (4)

_ _ _ _

2 Intelligent bishop leading Tories (6)

_ _ _ _ _ _

3 Odd Manx cat creating a disturbance (6)

_ _ _ _ _ _

4 Fruit and nuts (7)

_ _ _ _ _ _ _

5 Crook most active where provisions are kept (9)

_ _ _ _ _ _ _ _ _

A	A	A	B	B	C	G	H
H	I	K	M	M	M	N	N
N	O	O	O	P	R	R	R
S	S	S	T	T	U	U	Y

Cryptic Quintagrams®

125

1 Man, say, is left by fiancée finally (4)

— — — —

2 Attack traps this simpleton (7)

— — — — — — —

3 Dan and Irma Bowling's girl (7)

— — — — — — —

4 Got up to shoot enigmatic dying word in film (7)

— — — — — — —

5 On stage comes a learner — gutsy! (7)

— — — — — — —

A	A	A	B	D	D	E	E
E	E	G	G	I	I	I	L
L	M	M	N	N	N	O	R
R	R	S	S	T	U	U	

126

1 Chess piece in hand, knight (4)

— — — —

2 Alluring woman, in truth, our ideal (5)

— — — — —

3 Top hurdler, perhaps (6)

— — — — — —

4 Artisan less inclined to work after end of spring (7)

— — — — — — —

5 Penny-pincher, cold fish, saving pile (10)

— — — — — — — — — —

A	A	A	A	C	E	E	E
E	G	H	H	I	I	J	K
L	M	N	O	P	P	P	R
R	R	S	T	U	U	W	Z

Cryptic Quintagrams®

127

1 Separate — or almost do (4)

_ _ _ _

2 Family left in American gaol (4)

_ _ _ _

3 Waste a prize (7)

_ _ _ _ _ _ _

4 Substitute English placed in struggling side (8)

_ _ _ _ _ _ _ _

5 Standard pipe connector (male) (5,4)

_ _ _ _ _ _ _ _ _

A	A	A	A	C	C	D	E
E	H	I	I	J	K	L	N
N	N	O	O	P	P	P	R
R	S	T	T	T	U	U	Y

128

1 Time inside for example? (4)

_ _ _ _

2 House deposit (5)

_ _ _ _ _

3 Needing bed, notice outside shelter (6)

_ _ _ _ _ _

4 Obstacle on tour for musical group (7)

_ _ _ _ _ _ _

5 Good results I have — one after another (10)

_ _ _ _ _ _ _ _ _ _

A	C	C	D	E	E	E	E
E	E	G	I	I	L	L	L
O	P	P	R	S	S	S	S
S	T	T	T	U	V	Y	Y

Cryptic Quintagrams®

9 TALEA

a. A counting stick

b. Rhythm

c. A grass

11 TAOVALA

a. Semolina liquor

b. A board game

c. A sporran

b. To bluster

c. A sea-fis

16 BRETELLE

a. A shoulder-strap
b. A female Breton
c. Fermented black currant liquor

10 COLOPHONY

a. Part singing
b. Abdominal surgery

Word Watch

12 COMICES

a. An assembly

Lexica

Polygon

Quintagram®

Word Watch

Codeword

How to Play

Select the correct answer that defines the head word.

DEADOH
a. Drunk
b. Asleep
c. Dried flowers

DRAMBUIE
a. A breed of terrier
b. A whisky liqueur
c. A Highland plaid

WEATHERGALL
a. An imperfect rainbow
b. A storm-sail
c. A jelly-fish

VANDEMONIAN
a. A din of devils
b. Tasmanian
c. Sale by barter

1 **TALLAGE**
a. Height
b. A feudal tax
c. Candle-making

2 **JOINTURE**
a. Butchering of meat
b. A property settlement
c. Carpentry

3 **BELLETRIST**
a. A bell-maker
b. A fine writer
c. A dancer

4 **SPIRACLE**
a. A small spiral staircase
b. A minor conspiracy
c. A breathing hole

5 **AMENT**
a. A catkin
b. The final lines of a prayer
c. Loving

6 **TMESIS**
a. Adding in a word
b. Decay over time
c. A chemical reaction

7 **INSET**
a. A cabal
b. A training day
c. A pop-up window

8 **OBELION**
a. A fairground organ
b. Fish stew
c. Part of the skull

9 **QUILLET**
   a. A quibble
   b. A small quilt
   c. An 18th-century pen case

10 **REPUNIT**
   a. A repeated number
   b. Recriminatory
   c. A piece of pipe work

11 **SERVITE**
   a. Cringing
   b. Balkan pottery
   c. Member of a religious order

12 **TECKEL**
   a. A spin move in skating
   b. A dog
   c. To caress lightly

13 **PAVID**
   a. A flagstone
   b. Timid
   c. Flattened

14 **APAGOGE**
   a. The mid point of an orbit
   b. A fruit
   c. An indirect argument

15 **GOBANG**
   a. A Japanese board-game
   b. A warehouse
   c. A Khmer rice dish

16 **CATAPAN**
   a. A lover
   b. A litter tray
   c. A governor

17 **TOCOPHEROL**
   a. A vitamin
   b. Industrial alcohol
   c. A hormone

18 **GLUME**
   a. Darkness
   b. The outside of a blade of grass
   c. Poor-quality paste

19 **NACKET**
   a. A whale harpoon
   b. A notch
   c. A snack lunch

20 **STEEVE**
   a. A docker
   b. To raise a bowsprit
   c. Wool trimmings

21 **KENSPECKLE**
   a. Freckly
   b. Conspicuous
   c. To splash

22 **LAPIDOSE**
   a. Errant, careless
   b. Of a stony nature
   c. Blue-coloured

23 **MARCID**
   a. Withered
   b. Sour-tasting
   c. A Spanish wine

24 **NESTLECOCK**
   a. A codpiece
   b. A children's game
   c. A weakling

25 VERDIN
a. Stained green
b. A bird
c. Blossoming

26 SELD
a. Rare
b. Pompous
c. Silvered

27 MORSE
a. A heath shrub
b. Slight regret
c. A walrus

28 AVESTAN
a. Without light
b. Bird-shaped
c. Scriptural language

29 POGGY
a. A bogeyman
b. Plump
c. A small whale

30 MEW
a. A secret den
b. To shave
c. A blackhead or pimple

31 SWEEPAGE
a. Scavenged food
b. Hay
c. The right to collect wood

32 ESURIENT
a. Lazy
b. Greedy
c. Luxurious

33 VERTIBLE
a. Inconstant
b. Genuine
c. Inflammatory

34 SEPTICAL
a. Of the nose
b. Poisonous
c. in 7/7 time

35 HETHING
a. Scorn
b. Bullying
c. Panting

36 WEAL
a. To sob
b. A boundary stone
c. Riches

37 BAILOR
a. An owner
b. A leaky ship
c. To wail

38 BEVOR
a. To save
b. Hard worker
c. Armour

39 BELAR
a. A tree
b. Handsome
c. To vault

40 BEGAR
a. Bright
b. Labour
c. A tributary stream

41 KABADDI
a. A short club
b. A game of tag
c. A loin cloth

42 ZITI
a. Spotty
b. Pasta
c. A sequin

43 FAGOTTO
a. A bassoon
b. An Italian rissole
c. A type of singing

44 VENTURI
a. A privateer
b. A rivet
c. A measuring tube

45 SOAM
a. A pore
b. A chain on a horse
c. To smooth

46 SHAB
a. A knife handle
b. An itching disease
c. Dowdy

47 LEISTER
a. A spear
b. An overcoat
c. A cheese

48 DALLOP
a. A shapeless lump
b. A floppy hat
c. A meadow flower

49 DEGOMBLE
a. To clear
b. To snooze
c. A furry toy

50 SNITTERING
a. To shiver
b. A nap
c. Snowfall

51 FEEFLE
a. To swirl
b. Delicate
c. Hungover

52 HOGAMADOG
a. A sausage roll
b. A snowball
c. A sled dog

53 SNIT
a. Trimmed
b. To rat on
c. A fit of temper

54 TONDO
a. A companion
b. A painting
c. Crazy

55 SALLET
a. A helmet
b. A wooden support
c. Mixed green leaves

56 BUTTYMAN
a. A waterer of gardens
b. A sandwich-maker
c. A mining contractor

57 TROVER

a. A treasure-hunter

b. A ferret

c. Taking illegally

58 CHOWRI

a. A fried savoury

b. A fly whisk

c. A servant

59 BASENJI

a. The dog that didn't bark

b. A Chinese mushroom

c. A martial art

60 BICHIR

a. A fish

b. Muesli

c. To thrash

61 MAESTOSO

a. Quickly spreading

b. Majestically

c. In the manner of a master

62 WHERRY

a. A crossbreed dog

b. A whirlpool

c. A rowing boat

63 SARABANDE

a. A dance

b. An ornamental sash

c. A Hungarian sleigh

64 FRENUM

a. A priest's bowl

b. A fold of skin

c. A coin

65 THEORBO
a. A sighting device
b. A broadsword
c. A form of lute

66 THEREMIN
a. An electronic musical instrument
b. A sex hormone
c. A vitamin

67 DITHYRAMB
a. An irregular polygon
b. A drinking song
c. A metrical foot

68 AUSTRALORP
a. A chicken
b. A form of zither
c. Gold-bearing rock

69 LEMMA
a. Part of an argument
b. A female lemming
c. A shadow

70 LENTICULAR
a. Freckly
b. Lens-shaped
c. Relating to a fast

71 POILU
a. A chicken
b. Expensive flour
c. An infantryman

72 REJONEADOR
a. A cigar case
b. A mounted bullfighter
c. A religious ritual

73 WAYZGOOSE

a. A printers' holiday

b. Christmas leftovers

c. A traditional rhyme

74 SNAKEHEAD

a. An iron spike

b. A poisonous plant

c. A mountain pass

75 LEAGUER

a. A fast walker

b. A semi-professional cricketer

c. A liquid measure

76 GECK

a. Liver sausage

b. Unpleasant goo

c. A fool

77 EUTHERIAN

a. With a placenta

b. A medicinal herb

c. Legendary

78 MONODY

a. The quality of a dirge

b. A poem for one

c. A one-day event

79 ABERGLAUBE

a. A Welsh cheese

b. Glazed pottery

c. Superstition

80 PERISELENIUM

a. A food supplement

b. Lunar orbit

c. A fairy ring

81 KNOP
a. A knob
b. A small wood
c. A vegetable

82 PLANISHED
a. Filled up
b. Hammered
c. Electro-plated

83 EUTHENICS
a. Improving the environment
b. Improving human stock
c. Improving biology

84 PALANQUIN
a. A knight errant
b. A stuffed cushion
c. A covered litter

85 STONE
a. An organ pipe
b. A compositor's table
c. A low-scoring hand in euchre

86 PIGHTLE
a. A paddock
b. A piglet
c. A promise

87 EMMER
a. A strain of wheat
b. A tourist
c. A printer's ruler

88 RAMSTAM
a. Part of a musketeer's kit
b. Headlong
c. A champion sheep

89 FALCONET
a. A bird of prey
b. A field gun
c. A military cadet

90 ALIZARIN
a. Red dye
b. A Persian wizard
c. Spiced lentils

91 ROWEL
a. A farm wagon
b. A plant's burr
c. A spur wheel

92 SLEEVEEN
a. A cuff decoration
b. A smooth talker
c. Illicit spirits

93 ALEPH
a. A Hebrew letter
b. A prayer leader
c. A clay tablet

94 KANJI
a. Chinese letters
b. Hot sauce
c. Knotweed

95 ANABIOSIS
a. Living without air
b. Decontamination
c. Returning to life

96 VORANT
a. Devouring
b. A canopy
c. Criminal

7		12		6
	12	17 **N**	1	23
3		4 **A**		2
2		22	4	21
7		1		
4	13	6	2	4

Codeword

Word Watch   Quintagram®   Polygon   Lexica   Codeword

How to Play

Numbers are substituted for letters in the crossword grid.

Below the grid is the key. Some letters are solved.

When you have completed your first word or phrase you will have the clues to more letters.
Enter them in the key grid and the main grid and check the letters on the alphabet list as you
complete them.

A B C D E F G H I J K L M N Ø P Q Ŗ S T U V W X Y Z

1	2 R	3	4	5	6	7	8	9	10	11	12	13
14	15	16	17	18	19	20	21 O	22	23	24	25	26

245

1

4	24	22	11	21	8		16	7	7	15	17	22
	14		21		26		9		20		9	
25	16	17	4	21	10	8	10		9	15	21	26
	9		23		8		8		12		11	
20	26	24	21		11	20	9	6	16	9	20	11
			9		21					9		
	21	26	8	19	7 (C)	15	4	20	18	25	22	
	26						8		21			
4	1	15	8	8	5	8	10		25	16	18	8
	15		20		8		15 (U)		25		8	
2	8	4	24	18	8	7	13	16	26	8	10	
	4		8		9		8		3		7	
4	24	20	26	5	20		9	14	22 (Y)	24	14	11

A B Ȼ D E F G H I J K L M N O P Q R S T Ø V W X Ɏ Z

1	2	3	4	5	6	7 C	8	9	10	11	12	13
14	15 U	16	17	18	19	20	21	22 Y	23	24	25	26

2

	18		7		20		6		7		9	
18	1	17	19	2	22		12	14	14	15	22	4
	6		22		23		20		22		15	
26	1	12	25		19	2	2	3	12	9	15	15
	8				15		12		13		4	
16	12	21	12	22	4	15	1	7	8 **L**	25		
	22		14						2		7	
	12	14	14	15	17	17	15	4	12	20	2	
	12		22		5		2				1	
23	11	24	2	7	20	2	4		14	1	9 **B**	2
	10		4		12		8		15		9	
9	23 **I**	3	23	11	23		2	4	23	9	8	2
	8		20		8		25		11		25	

A B̸ C D E F G H I̸ J K L̸ M N O P Q R S T U V W X Y Z

1	2	3	4	5	6	7	8 **L**	9 **B**	10	11	12	13
14	15	16	17	18	19	20	21	22	23 **I**	24	25	26

3

5	19	24	5	21		2	24	23	2	15	6	11
25		6		9		10		3		14		2
15	2	6	24	13	2	8 **D**		15	14	21	12	24
9		3		2				9				15
6	3	16	2	15	2	8		6	9	12	2	6
6		24				15		6		14		11
	9	10	2	17	14	9	7	24	12	6	11	
22		26		14		2				6		24
24	15	2	10	24		8	9	18	9	8	2	8
5				26				3		3		21
7	25	24	10	1		4	24	26	14	20	20	9
2		8		2		24		24		2		15
15	2	3 **O**	15	8	2	15		6	24	15	23	2

A B C Ø E F G H I J K L M N Ø P Q R S T U V W X Y Z

1	2	3 **O**	4	5	6	7	8 **D**	9	10	11	12	13
14	15	16	17	18	19	20	21	22	23	24	25	26

248

4

7		25	24	8	2		4	13	8	20		11
1	16	13			24		24			13	8	6
1		21		10	13	6	8	20		15		7
26	9	26	8		20		24		22	6	8	20
15		23		9	3	2 **Y**	21	6		11		3
	17	6	20	24		26		8	21	24	14	
			7	11	17	6	9	8	6			
	9	7	14	6		16		7 **A**	18	9	2	
4		19		24	11	11	16	2		6		20
16	26	7	9		9		13		24	17	6	9 **R**
26		16		18	26	8	25	2		24		13
8	6	6			1		26			5	26	20
8		7	13	12	20		12	7	21	6		3

A̸ B C D E F G H I J K L M N O P Q R̸ S T U V W X Y̸ Z

1	2 **Y**	3	4	5	6	7 **A**	8	9 **R**	10	11	12	13
14	15	16	17	18	19	20	21	22	23	24	25	26

5

4	8	10	21	26	14	■	8	10	11 **F**	11	26	15
■	22	■	22	■	26	■	6	■	22	■	11	■
26	3	22	14	1	4	2	26	■	8	4	11	26
■	3	■	13	■	6	■	26	■	10	■	26	■
25	22 **O**	3	2	■	26	7	5	22	13	10	6	26
■	16	■	26	■	13	■	■	■	■	■	18	■
2	10	6	6	26	2	■	13	23	4	12	26	15
■	17	■	■	■	■	■	26	■	21	■	13	■
5	4	17	14	2	9	22	7	■	4	6	8 **C**	20
■	3	■	17	■	10	■	2	■	19	■	26	■
24	17	14	1	■	1	6	4	15	17	26	14	2
■	13	■	20	■	1	■	14	■	14	■	8	■
13	21	17	2	20	12	■	2	10	1	1	26	15

A B C̸ D E F̸ G H I J K L M N Ø P Q R S T U V W X Y Z

1	2	3	4	5	6	7	8 **C**	9	10	11 **F**	12	13
14	15	16	17	18	19	20	21	22 **O**	23	24	25	26

6

25	20	23	8	25	8	11	26	■	9	16	12	12
8	■	21	■	12	■	19	■	18	■	12	■	2
9	7	2	12	13	■	16	21	21	17	9	21	19
12	■	8	■	12	■	8	■	1	■	16	■	15
13	21	21	26	■	11	9	15	22	22	21	16	23
■	■	15	■	10	■	12	■	21	■	■	■	1
14	12	11	9	12	16	■	26	21	15	11	11	12
7	■	■	■	12	■	7	■	3	■	5	■	■
25	6	12	12	16 **R**	8	18	20	■	9	15	23	7
3	■	16	■	8	■	3	■	9	■	7	■	19
19	8	16	7	23	6	7	■	15	23	18	12	9 **T**
21	■	21	■	1	■	18	■	22	■	8	■	18
9	7	16	23	■	4	8	24	7	16	13	16	20

A B C D E F G H I J K L M N O P Q ~~R~~ S ~~T~~ U V W X Y Z

1	2	3	4	5	6	7	8	9 **T**	10	11	12	13
14	15	16 **R**	17	18	19	20	21	22	23	24	25	26

7

	7		15		18		15		3		12
19	11	5	13	26	19	26	14		13	10	13	19
	17		26		2		21		26		24	
1	19	14	7	21	26 **N**		2	7	9	21	15	20
			14		19				19		14	
7	15	15	7	23	17	14		3	24 **Y**	26	21	3
	14				15		4				3	
5	2	21	25	19		8	21	26	21	3	18	24
	23		19				15		1			
7	16	20	7	15	14		14	2	19	6	13	2
	16		17		15		8		7		4	
7	17	14	13 **O**		7	22	23	21	17	21	26	19
	19		14		2		17		15		15	

A B C D E F G H I J K L M N̸ Ø P Q R S T U V W X Y̸ Z

1	2	3	4	5	6	7	8	9	10	11	12	13 **O**
14	15	16	17	18	19	20	21	22	23	24 **Y**	25	26 **N**

252

8

	7	15	2	26	26		22	11	15	17 H	16	
3		11		11		18		6		4		9
4	12	12		3	12	16	6	26		24	2	24
16		18				26				24		7
15	17	9	15		25	16	1		18	16	9	1
17			12	16	19		4	22	2			9
15	11	26	16 A		26		25		9	12	11	24
11			20	11	11		9	26	26			15
22 M	16	24	19		24	11	14		1	4	8	1
3		11			24				4			9
4	16	1		7	5	2	16	14		12	4	21
12		15		9		7		2		9		4
	6	17	16	12	23		10	11	13	4	14	

A B C D E F G H I J K L M N O P Q R S T U V W X Y Z

1	2	3	4	5	6	7	8	9	10	11	12	13
14	15	16 A	17 H	18	19	20	21	22 M	23	24	25	26

9

10	25	9	5	18	14	2	■	4	14	23	23	13 **L**
22	■	18	■	25	■	22	■	14	■	15	■	25
4	13	18	25	19	■	2	7	22	11	22	9	2
17	■	17	■	21	■	7	■	26	■	4	■	19
20	5	2	12	25	5	23	19	■	2	19	22	24
22	■	■	14	■	2	■	6	■	13	■	■	
26	5	2	23	2	19	■	13	22	26	24	23	14
■	■	9	■	19	■	21	■	25	■	■	■	23
21	18	18 **O**	9	■	13	18	13	13	5	8	18	8
23	■	18	■	13	■	25	■	19	■	13	■	14
6	5	1	1	5	9	16	■	5	11	22	16	18
18	■	23	■	20	■	7	■	23	■	5	■	3
16	25	2	19	18	■	2	24	14	5	9	16	23

A B C D E F G H I J K L̸ M N Ø P Q R S T U V W X Y Z

| 1 | 2 | 3 | 4 | 5 | 6 | 7 | 8 | 9 | 10 | 11 | 12 | 13 **L** |
| 14 | 15 | 16 | 17 | 18 **O** | 19 | 20 | 21 | 22 | 23 | 24 | 25 | 26 |

254

10

	24	18	20	3	23	6	19		18	8	2	23
23		22		20		14		17		18		11
2	20	10	4	18	19	14		2	20	16	3	17
19		4		14		4		1		6		4
12	3	14 D	1	4		9	4	20	3	6	19	
6				21		23		18		7		1
3	20	5	15	2	25		6	22	23	18	26	4
15		15		18		14		3				6
	8	2	9	23 T	15	4		6	5	5	18	15
12		4		4		15		2		19		6
18	20	20	2	15		2 U	17	9	13	3	20	1
9		22		11		14		15		15		11
9	23	11	4		19	4	22	11	22	15	4	

A B C Ø E F G H I J K L M N O P Q R S ⁄ Ø V W X Y Z

1	2 U	3	4	5	6	7	8	9	10	11	12	13
14 D	15	16	17	18	19	20	21	22	23 T	24	25	26

11

23	8	2	5	16	18		7	13	9	8	2	15
10		21		23			11		14			24
24	1	12	2	8	15	23		25	17	23	26	4
8		24		2		24		23		5		23
5	7	23	23	5		2	8	2	13	5	18	
23			23		21				23			
15	13	19	13	11 **N**	12		25	23	24	15	8	17
		13			6		22					21
	3	26	18	5	16	23		16	18	23	11	8
21		5		8		23		24		11		5
1	2	21	7	17		2	23	20	8	5	26	16 **H**
24		2		21				23		23		23
3	1	18 **Y**	13	11	12		8	15	21	2	23	15

A B C D E F G H̷ I J K L M N̷ O P Q R S T U V W X Y̷ Z

1	2	3	4	5	6	7	8	9	10	11 **N**	12	13
14	15	16 **H**	17	18 **Y**	19	20	21	22	23	24	25	26

256

12

13	24	8	8	11	23	■	11	8	9	2	23	6
16	■	24	■	3			11	■	23	■	11	
2	13	13	11	16		11	26	12	2	23	7	11
16	■	16	■	14		3		14	■	14	■	26
24	1	20	12	12	24	18		1	14	4	11	12
18	■	22		■		2		24			■	20
■		11	17	19	24	10	14	18	2	12 (L)		■
5		■		26		2			11		2	
19	26	18 (C)	19	16		16	14	19	23	24	13	16
8	■	12		4		14		26	■	13	■	16
9	23	2	21	24	11	23		18	23	19	1	11
12	■	26		13		■		12		23	■	26
11	24	7	25	16	25	■	1	11	15	11	26	1

A B C̸ D E F G H I J K L̸ M N O P Q R S T U V W X Y Z

1	2	3	4	5	6	7	8	9	10	11	12 **L**	13
14	15	16	17	18 **C**	19	20	21	22	23	24	25	26

13

14	10	21	24	16		6 **R**	10	18	24	16		3
	4			21	25	7		23		17	10	7
1 **V**	7	6	13	7		20	10	2	7	6		6
21		7				23		21		10		8
24	16	6	7	24	24	12	23	26		20	18	9
16		23		23		12		21			21	
18	11	19	21	19	13		13	18	15	23	14	5
	17			24		8		6		1		21
24	10	20		25	18	19	4	9	16	23	12	16
22		6		6		10				26		17
23		18	13	7	19	16		10	1	18	6	9
18	24	24		7		16	10	6			18	
16		24	18	19	4	9		20 **B**	21	19	13	10

A B̸ C D E F G H I J K L M N O P Q R̸ S T U V̸ W X Y Z

| 1 **V** | 2 | 3 | 4 | 5 | 6 **R** | 7 | 8 | 9 | 10 | 11 | 12 | 13 |
| 14 | 15 | 16 | 17 | 18 | 19 | 20 **B** | 21 | 22 | 23 | 24 | 25 | 26 |

14

25	6	23	23	14	26	7	5	■	14	25 **B**	21	3
22	■	17	■	2	■	17	■	5	■	14	■	16
22	15	8	3	18	■	5	8	12	1	8	17	2
20	■	10	■	3	■	22	■	20	■	22	■	3
5	10	3	7	■	8	13	22	1	3	18	2	3
■	■	26	■	7	■	18	■	8	■	■	■	7
9	17	5	5	3	5	■	2	22	5	20	22	5
17	■	■	20	■	20	■	20	■	14	■	■	■
21	3	15	8	22	11	3	26	■	4	26	17	8
21	■	3	■	18	■	26	■	18	■	14	■	22
19	6	20 **M**	1	17	18	4	■	22	16	25	22	13
22	■	6	■	2	■	3	■	22	■	22	■	3
12	14	26	7	■	8	26	14 **A**	18	24	6	17	21

~~A~~ ~~B~~ C D E F G H I J K L ~~M~~ N O P Q R S T U V W X Y Z

1	2	3	4	5	6	7	8	9	10	11	12	13
14 **A**	15	16	17	18	19	20 **M**	21	22	23	24	25 **B**	26

15

	1	17	8	3 M	21		17	25	3	21	17	
14		13		20		1		19		15		6
18	13	26	20	4		21	18	25	17	22	25	10
8		21		14		8		5		22		8
6	10	20	9	13	8	18		17	18	20	5	2
6		17				4		25				25
	1	16	13	9	25		20	23	3	15	17	
1				15		25				4		17
21 P	20	4	15	5		7	8	15	5	2	10	12
15		12		15		8		4		10		21
17	13	3	24	13	10	20		25	11	15	10	25
25		21		8		10		21		4		23
	5	16	20	1	3		1	17	20	14	25	

A B C D E F G H I J K L M̸ N O P̸ Q R S T U V W X Y Z

1	2	3 M	4	5	6	7	8	9	10	11	12	13
14	15	16	17	18	19	20	21 P	22	23	24	25	26

260

20	15	13	6	17 R	26		10	14	17	9	14	7
15		6		23				1		15		17
11	6	15		24	14	21	4	20 I	22	6	3	14
5		16		14		6		4				21
17	6	4	21		21	1	3	23	21	2 H	14	21
10		20		6		14		1		23		26
		5	18	15	14	17	21	2	20	1		
25		15		14		2		21		2		23
6	15	21	2	23	8	14	15		10	23	20	15
20				17		17		6		19		15
11	17	23	16	4	20	5	6	21		23	12	14
11		17		2			14		17		12
21	23	10	5	21	23		7	17	14	7	9	14

A B C D E F G H̸ I̸ J K L M N O P Q R̸ S T U V W X Y Z

1	2 H	3	4	5	6	7	8	9	10	11	12	13
14	15	16	17 R	18	19	20 I	21	22	23	24	25	26

2	6	25	25	18	23	2	6	■	7	23	4	17
25	■	8	■	25	■	9	■	2	■	20	■	23
1	6	25	25	14	■	20	23	18	■	7	23	10
11	■	■	■	6	■	22	■	23	■	4	■	■
■	11	16	24	13	■	13	2	11	16	9	20	22
19	■	26	■	18	4	25	13	■	■	25	■	9
9	20	25	13	2	8	■	21	13	4	20	9	11
13	■	14	■	■	14	13	20	11	■	12	■	8
22	25	2	23	14	25	22 **D**	■	11	16	13	22	■
■	■	6	■	9	■	3	■	25	■	■	■	2
13	24	16	■	5	16	16	■	17	16	9 **U**	20	11
14	■	16	■	8	■	23	■	18	■	2	■	13
1	23	11	8	■	15	20	23	11 **T**	21	25	13	14

A B C Ø E F G H I J K L M N Ö P Q R S ⁄ Ø V W X Y Z

1	2	3	4	5	6	7	8	9 **U**	10	11 **T**	12	13
14	15	16	17	18	19	20	21	22 **D**	23	24	25	26

18

	3	12	26	19	13	2		16	19	20 D	12	
16		13		20		20		14		19		25
26	19	20	2	9		4	23	8	3	13	12	17
23		23		12		8		2		12		7
23	13	7	2	3	20	16		9	2	3	6	2
21		12				26		23				17
	2	20	2	5	12		21	3	23	16	12	
24				3		2				18		19
15	19	21 P	21	23		5	3	2	1	19	13	5
12		8		2		3		9		26		9
12	10	21	2	13	16	12		23	8	26	20	23
22		21		12		12		23		12		23
	20	17	12	20		20	12	11	19	13	12	

A B C Ø E F G H I J K L M N O Ø Q R S T U V W X Y Z

1	2	3	4	5	6	7	8	9	10	11	12	13
14	15	16	17	18	19	20 D	21 P	22	23	24	25	26

19

	8	14	7	2	20	4		12	24	5 (V)	21	
1		17		5		13		22		2		1
13	12	5	8	12		12	15	14	2	25	12	13
8		20		13		17		20		12		3
19	13	2	19	19	12	13		2	16	20	12	4
12		5				21		3				12
	15	17	9	2 (O)	13		8	19	19	12	13	
10				24		26				6		3
20 (L)	21	3	24	16		11	8	17	26	7	12	4
3		24		2		8		20		12		12
6	17	14	26	3	18	12		1	17	20	26	17
23		8		24		17		8		2		20
	26	19	17	16		23	3	15	2	24	2	

A B C D E F G H I J K L̸ M N Ø P Q R S T U ¥ W X Y Z

1	2 O	3	4	5 V	6	7	8	9	10	11	12	13
14	15	16	17	18	19	20 L	21	22	23	24	25	26

20

5	1	9	6	22	4		7		21	1	10	13
11		6		1		7	1	18	25			19
8	3	18	1	26	9		9		4	3 **O**	9	6
9			11		15		5		19			9
25	2	23	25	17	17	1	12	25		1	19	25
		6			18		6		9			8
23	6	18 **P**	13	3	19		14	11	25	6	17	4
3		1		26		6			22			
7	1	13		23	3	26	16	11	19	1	26	9 **G**
17		6		25		8		18				3
24	11	10	10		20		11	18	19	3	6	19
25			3	26	11	17		25		10		17
8	11	23	13		19		8	19	11	8	9	25

A B C D E F G̶ H I J K L M N O̶ P̶ Q R S T U V W X Y Z

| 1 | 2 | 3 **O** | 4 | 5 | 6 | 7 | 8 | 9 **G** | 10 | 11 | 12 | 13 |
| 14 | 15 | 16 | 17 | 18 **P** | 19 | 20 | 21 | 22 | 23 | 24 | 25 | 26 |

21

8	20	23 **R**	22	17	23	24		20	11	18	13	23
17		13		20		19		26		23		20
10	1	7	17	12		16	4	1	26	1	26	5
1		1		5		26		12		5		18
17	8	8	20	23	23	13	14		25	19	26	24
20				17		14		10		26		
22	21	20	19	16	2		22	7	20	14	5	13
		10		26		13		13				12
9	19	16	26		13	6	8	19	15	19	12	13
13		19		3		17		22		23		23
15 **V**	13	23	14	1	8	12		19	14	17	23	26
13		14		7		1		26		11		19
23	13	22	13	12		8	19	12	8	19	7	7

A B C D E F G H I J K L M N O P Q ~~R~~ S T U ~~V~~ W X Y Z

1	2	3	4	5	6	7	8	9	10	11	12	13
14	15 **V**	16	17	18	19	20	21	22	23 **R**	24	25	26

266

22

3	22	18	14	1 V	17		12	25	18	5	17	7
25		15		18		14		15		15		4
26	18	15	18	16	13	17		6	2	4	14	7
17		4		18		8		21		24		19
14	18	20	4	15		18	3	22	14	21	7	17
10				16		23				15		7
	1	21	15	20	8		25	3	18	19	17	
4		15				3		17				21
1	21	1	21	7	8	20 Y		21	7	21	4	9
17		4		21		14		11		15 N		26
14	25	8	17	14		25	5	25	8	17	8	17
7		1		19		26		14		14		7
4	26	17	15	17	14		10	17	17	22	8	17

A B C D E F G H I J K L M N̸ O P Q R S T U V̸ W X Y̸ Z

1 V	2	3	4	5	6	7	8	9	10	11	12	13
14	15 N	16	17	18	19	20 Y	21	22	23	24	25	26

23

15	■	20	■	6	■	7	■	14	■	1	■	1
3	17	7	16	6	20	14	6	9	■	12	11	5
3	■	11	■	23	■	22	■	22	■	3	■	14
2	3	12	20	3	12	13	■	19	18	10	18	20
16	■	■	■	■	16	■	■	■	2	■	1
3	16	15	■	15 **F**	16	3	17	14	2	16	3	■
12	■	6	■	11	■	■	■	22	■	3	■	16
■	22	6	12	8	18	12	6	21	■	8	21	3
25	■	1	■	■	3	■	■	■	■	■	9
11	2	19	6	12	■	20	3	12	24	14 **I**	9	4
18	■	6	■	14	■	22	■	6	■	12	■	1
9	14	16 **L**	■	20	26	18	3	11	10	14	20	19
1	■	8	■	13	■	3	■	10	■	20	■	21

A B C D E F̸ G H I̸ J K L̸ M N O P Q R S T U V W X Y Z

1	2	3	4	5	6	7	8	9	10	11	12	13
14 **I**	15 **F**	16 **L**	17	18	19	20	21	22	23	24	25	26

24

20	3	14	22	9	11		22	13	23	22	25	21
2		12		20				16		4		3
13	22	10		22	23	3	5	18	6	21	18	19
8		3		8		18		21				20
3	19	9	20		1	19	22	6	4	21	10	21
10		3		1		8		21		26		8
		16	1	19	21	16	4	22	19	20 H		
23		12		22		7		23		22		1
22	1	1	16	8	19	21	10		17	12	3	4
24				11		8		1		1		20
15	3	18	5	21	8	19 T	3	4		19	16	21
12		3		8				12		21		8
23	22	19	21	1	19		15	8	3	10	5	21

A B C D E F G H́ I J K L M N O P Q R S T́ U V W X Y Z

1	2	3	4	5	6	7	8	9	10	11	12	13
14	15	16	17	18	19 T	20 H	21	22	23	24	25	26

269

25

25	3	4	3	24	18	■	4	24	9	10	18	21
■	25	■	26	■	24	■	11	■	11	■	11	■
15	24	22	22	3	7	3	19	■	18	5	16	10
■	9	■	5	■	6	■	20	■	24	■	10	■
2	3	24	25	■	14	7	24	16	25	24	5	19
■	■	■	3	■	11	■	■	■	■	■	3	■
■	3	18	19 D	3	25	16 F	18 L	11	12	3	25	■
■	8	■	■	■	■	11	■	24	■	■	■	■
23	14	7	17	10	5	11	7	■	18	5	9	22
■	3	■	11	■	7	■	6	■	10	■	17	■
10	25	5	1	■	19	25	5	13	13	18	3	19
■	25	■	3	■	3	■	7	■	3	■	7	■
9	21	7	10	24	26	■	6	24	19	6	3	10

A B C Ð E F́ G H I J K Ľ M N O P Q R S T U V W X Y Z

1	2	3	4	5	6	7	8	9	10	11	12	13
14	15	16 F	17	18 L	19 D	20	21	22	23	24	25	26

270

26

	17		25		5		24 **C**		11		9	
16	23	5	6	4	23		5 **L**	18	13	18	26	12
	4		14		2		20		17		18	
19	5	18	11		6	21	16 **S**	18	5	23	9	11
	20				11		11		6		1	
20	4	11	26	17	26	20	22	18	24	11		
	23		11						6		6	
		16	1	20	17	3	6	9	9	6	21	19
	16		11		5		21				11	
23	7	18	23	26	6	18	10		10	23	26	8
	18		9		21		23		20		9	
15	6	22	11	16	9		9	23	24	9	6	24
	14		22		1		11		8		23	

A B ¢ D E F G H I J K Ł M N O P Q R $ T U V W X Y Z

1	2	3	4	5 **L**	6	7	8	9	10	11	12	13
14	15	16 **S**	17	18	19	20	21	22	23	24 **C**	25	26

27

16	15	3	3	18		22	15	12	5	13	15	23
15		15		1		9		8		24		15
3	15	8	4	24	9	26		2	8	1	16	18 **Y**
5		15		8				21				11 **L**
2	16	12	2	25	1	8		25	15	21	7	15
16		19				15		1		1		18
	4	24	9	25	26	2	1	16	2	16	10	
25		26		9		25				25		9
26	19	9	2	8		9	6	2	25	26	9	13
15				17				13		8		2
16	1	7	11	9		19	15	18	11	1	20	26
14		8		8		24		11		24		1
15	16	15	11	18	25	26		11	1	25	9	8

A B C D E F G H I J K L̸ M N O P Q R S T U V W X Y̸ Z

1	2	3	4	5	6	7	8	9	10	11 **L**	12	13
14	15	16	17	18 **Y**	19	20	21	22	23	24	25	26

272

28

24		7	20	21	8		17	12	2	18		14
23	25	12			10		24			2	18	18
24		4		25	5	20	6	9		11		12
5	12	21	8		20		20		17	24	16	16
25		12		25 **P**	18	24	15	17		20		8
	17 **B**	18	24	5 **R**		10		8	12	5	10	
			23	12	18	2	8	10	1			
	23	1	8	26		20		22	8	8	22	
23		24		10	12	10	10	9		19		4
1	8	6	1		13		9		14	20	12	18
24		8		5	20	20	15	9		21		2
22	2	22			20		25			8	18	15
9		20	15	2	1		3	2	10	22		17

A B̷ C D E F G H I J K L M N O P̷ Q R̷ S T U V W X Y Z

1	2	3	4	5 **R**	6	7	8	9	10	11	12	13
14	15	16	17 **B**	18	19	20	21	22	23	24	25 **P**	26

29

12	18	11	3	24	8		7	10	19	20	3	19
	11		26		24		24		13		26	
16	3	9	25	11	9	3	1		24	5	13	3
	12		10		24		3		23		17	
12	21	24	2		10 **O**	11	21	20 **W**	3	17	14	4 **H**
	17		3		8						4	
22	10	26	1	11	3		9	3	6	10	21	3
	26						3		24		3	
12	26	10	20	1	9	10	16		14	10	26	14
	24		4		3		11		3		6	
8	17	20	17		24	21	21	3	26	1	3	3
	9		12		1		3		21		26	
15	3	12	21	9	2		1	3	24	9	21	4

A B C D E F G H̸ I J K L M N Ø P Q R S T U V W̸ X Y Z

1	2	3	4 **H**	5	6	7	8	9	10 **O**	11	12	13
14	15	16	17	18	19	20 **W**	21	22	23	24	25	26

274

30

18	21	1	17	19	1	14	21		1	26	14	11
8		26		24		11		6		6		5
23	7	26	23	21		2	23	16 **M**	9 **D**	14	6	25
24		23		10		1		7		2		11
9	24	18	10		3	14	23	24	21	24	6	7
		11		16		9		13				18
21	24	9	24	11	9		20	23	16	13	17	11
19				14		13		18		6		
24	7	3	1	16	6	23	18		6	7	23	18
21		17		1		14		3		1		24
26	14	11	12	24	26	11		1	7	7	11	5
10		26		9		1		19		15		21
22	6	4	11		8	23	1	7	9	1	14	22

A B C Ø E F G H I J K L M N O P Q R S T U V W X Y Z

1	2	3	4	5	6	7	8	9 **D**	10	11	12	13
14	15	16 **M**	17	18	19	20	21	22	23	24	25	26

31

	4		6		11		14		18		10	
22	20	8	22	19	23	24	6		17	5	14	6
	22		17		17		17		20		13	
20	1	1	17	8	17		4	17	16	14	13	17
			15		18				19		16	
5	20	23	6	12	17	6		6	25	23 **R**	2 **I**	15 **P**
	7				6		15				1	
25	2	15	6	21		16	2	25	14	23	13	21
	20		9				20		1			
6	25	23	14	5	6		1	2	26	24	17	16
	19		2		19		2		16		7	
13	23	20	1		3	17	6	25	17	23	17	4
	6		25		25		25		6		1	

A B C D E F G H I/J K L M N O P Q R S T U V W X Y Z

1	2 **I**	3	4	5	6	7	8	9	10	11	12	13
14	15 **P**	16	17	18	19	20	21	22	23 **R**	24	25	26

32

	17	26	12	11	21		14	10 W	7	7	22 D	
20		12		16		14		7		3 N		11
9	8	3		17	19	9	12	22		17	7	12
17		16				14				9		8
14	9	8	5		17	9	3		4	7	12	14
13			13	3	3		7	26	9			10
5	9	2	2		13		10		8	9	17	23
13			2	13	4		7	15	15			7
12	10	12	24		7	12	8		7	1	17	7
6		4				9				13		1
1	13	4		14	23	8	16	10		18	13	7
24		1		16		12		12		13		22
	3	24	1	16	3		7	25	9	22	7	

A B C Ø E F G H I J K L M Ŋ O P Q R S T U V Ŵ X Y Z

1	2	3 N	4	5	6	7	8	9	10 W	11	12	13
14	15	16	17	18	19	20	21	22 D	23	24	25	26

277

33

22	6	5	26	15	6	16		23	1	11	11	4
19		6		14		14		6		6		16
21	16	4	21	20		21	13	1	19	17	15	21
10		21		16		15		5		8		14
24	14	15	15	14	5	14	7		9	14	15	21
1				21		5		16		4		
18	19	8	10	15	21		8	4	18	18	6	16
		4		21		6		19				1
7	6	2	23		22	5	4	17	8 **G**	18 **L**	14	5
14		4		15		19		15		6		3
25	1	17	15	19	17	8		25	4	15	10	14
15		19		17		19		6		15		23
21	11	4	5	23		17	6	12	19	6	1	21

A B C D E F G̸ H I J K L̸ M N O P Q R S T U V W X Y Z

1	2	3	4	5	6	7	8 **G**	9	10	11	12	13
14	15	16	17	18 **L**	19	20	21	22	23	24	25	26

34

	2	19	6	5	7	23	13		23	25	6	3
25		1		14		5		19		16		25
8 (S)	24 (C)	19	7 (T)	7	23	5		11	3	25	8	8
12		23		3		17		6		20		9
7	6	25	3	25		25	24	2	19	6	7	
3				1		13		19		21		3
25	26	26	3	25	13		22	6	15	15	23	5
13		25		15		3		7				4
	8	7	3	25	26	5		18	24	24	19	3
7		25		21		11		19		18		25
3	5	23	6	24		19	21	8	24	3	5	17
6		23		5		10		23		25		21
18	21	13	14		3	5	24	13	24	23	5	

A B ¢ D E F G H I J K L M N O P Q R $ 𝑇 U V W X Y Z

1	2	3	4	5	6	7 **T**	8 **S**	9	10	11	12	13
14	15	16	17	18	19	20	21	22	23	24 **C**	25	26

35

26	4	4	2	22	2		8	26	5	1	23	26
10		2		23				4		15		1
26	17	17	15	9	23	26		4	18	9	1	7
5		15		5		16		15		3		2
7 H	23	9 N	22 G	2		26	5	21	4	18	17	
2			9		25			2				
19	25	18	19	22	2		17	2	13	25	23	1
		9			26		11					15
	26	25	13	8	18	4		13	25	26	17	12
5		26		15		5		25		17		23
24	26	6	2	25		15	25	2	22	26	9	15
15		2		22				17		14		18
13	26	4	20	2	19		25	2	1	2	5	5

A B C D E F G̸ H̸ I J K L M N̸ O P Q R S T U V W X Y Z

1	2	3	4	5	6	7 H	8	9 N	10	11	12	13
14	15	16	17	18	19	20	21	22 G	23	24	25	26

36

13	25	4	10	25	4		2	17	17	13	25	8
1		25		15			2		16		23
23	16	13	25	8		9	21	4	4	20	24	6
21		8		4		23		5		14		6
3	21	22	3	21	4	12		23	24	8	20	25
11		14				20		14				12
		25	15	16	25	26	8	21	24	8		
17				4		20				25		8
4	2	12	25	2		2	19	14	20	1	23	25
20		4		10		23		21		23		25
7	25	21	14	2	23	13		8 T	3	20	13	8
7		3		11				25		14		18
22	25	14	14	25	12		25	15 X	18	21	14	25

A B C D E F G H I J K L M N O P Q R S T̸ U V W X̸ Y Z

1	2	3	4	5	6	7	8 T	9	10	11	12	13
14	15 X	16	17	18	19	20	21	22	23	24	25	26

37

ABCDEFGHIJKLMNOPQRSTUVWXYZ

1	2	3	4	5	6	7	8	9	10	11	12 P	13
14 R	15	16	17	18	19	20	21	22	23	24 D	25	26

38

19	8	19	26	12	19	9	20		13	17	11	23
8		8		21		7		15		12		19
24	19	3	22	3		3	8	14	3	1	19	13
15		5		21		19		18		10		6
20	3	15	17		10	17	11	12	7	15	7	15
		13		10		21		21				5
22	12	9	9	3	17		21	9	15	23	24	3
12				3		17		21		17		
25 F	11	11	9 T	21	24	11	22 G		20	3	24	23
25		4		16		13		21		9		12
15	2	11	13	15	14	11		12	8	4	19	23
16		8		5		13		17		3		23
21	3	3	17		18	11	20	25	12	24	24	20

A B C D E F G H I J K L M N O P Q R S T U V W X Y Z

1	2	3	4	5	6	7	8	9 T	10	11	12	13
14	15	16	17	18	19	20	21	22 G	23	24	25 F	26

39

	6	22	23	20	16		21	20	24	1	5	
3		26		10		4		3		23 **H**		3
23	20	18	22	20		21	15	9	4	6	18	8
26		17		22		21		4		1 **K**		4
13	23	15	3	8	25	20		15	16	15	26	12
18		22				24		24				21
	3	8	26	26	16		23	20	16	14	20	
4				24		26				5		20
3	25	6	18	14		7	25	4	12	12	26	19
4		18		6		7		12		3		21
6	3	1	6	18	22	20		11	4	25	14	20
25		25		2		24		20		15		25
	24	20	25	6	19		22	24	5	21	8	

A B C D E F G H̸ I J K̸ L M N O P Q R S T U V W X Y Z

1 **K**	2	3	4	5	6	7	8	9	10	11	12	13
14	15	16	17	18	19	20	21	22	23 **H**	24	25	26

11	4	14	22	22	25	■	18 (C)	21 (H)	3	25	8	19
4	■	20	■	12	■	■	■	3	■	17	■	20
3	15	18	■	19	25	25	19	20	8	14	3	12
15	■	15	■	16	■	18	■	2 (D)	■	■	■	14
8	14	19	25	■	22	14	25	25	4	15	19	25
10	■	3	■	3	■	19	■	6	■	19	■	8
■	■	25	8	15	6	20	5	23	3	20	■	■
1	■	19	■	13	■	8	■	19	■	6	■	3
21	14	25	8	6	15	14	18	■	7	4	23	26
3	■	■	■	15	■	25	■	14	■	20	■	3
18	6	20	9	19	15	8	19	2	■	18	6	8
17	■	6	■	3	■	■	■	19	■	19	■	21
25	8	15	6	12	12	■	21	3	15	2	12	24

A B ₵ Ð E F G Ħ I J K L M N O P Q R S T U V W X Y Z

1	2 D	3	4	5	6	7	8	9	10	11	12	13
14	15	16	17	18 C	19	20	21 H	22	23	24	25	26

41

5	10	18	8	1	10	24	21		7	1	19	4
6		6		19 **R**		9		24		20		10
19	22	14	14	10		19	6	21		17	22	23
17			8 **G**		10		22		8			
	22	19	10	22		15	4	8	10	15	24	21
21		15		23 **M**	22	13	15			18		9
19	6	24	21	10	2		22	25	3	22	2	22
15		1			23	1	25	15		21		18
15	11	6	22	21	15	4		22	16	15	19	
		18		19		4		4				26
1	25	4		1	4	15		10	24	24	6	15
12		15		4		24		18		3		24
25	6	4	1		24	21	22	8	18	22	18	21

A B C D E F G H I J K L M N O P Q R S T U V W X Y Z

1	2	3	4	5	6	7	8 **G**	9	10	11	12	13
14	15	16	17	18	19 **R**	20	21	22	23 **M**	24	25	26

42

	6	12	12	6	10	26		12	13	26	20	
19		13		24		10		9		13		10
13	14	26	2	18		22	2	10	25	14	2	16
1		18		2		18		14		25		2
18	5	6	16	16	26	2		6	3	2	14	6
2		14				16		24				26
	4	6	14	8	1		12	11	1	5	7	
18				1		1				3		10
2	17	2	3	18		4 **B**	13	21 **Z**	21	6	3	16
15		9		18		26		2		14		26
9	3	1	23	10	12	1		4	13	25	26	2
1		24		14		14		3		26		16
	18	11	13	25		25	3	6	21	2	16	

A B̶ C D E F G H I J K L M N O P Q R S T U V W X Y Z̶

1	2	3	4 **B**	5	6	7	8	9	10	11	12	13
14	15	16	17	18	19	20	21 **Z**	22	23	24	25	26

287

43

	22	21	21	18	21	8		21	3	12	13	
23		1		5		12		11		7		25
13	12	17	12	25		3	12	25	5	13	13	24
15		18		12		12		18		15		10
10	13	24	4	15	15	8		5	6	15	3	21
21		10				21		17				8
	12	25	17	2	24		23	25	5	1 N	14	
23				15		9				19 U		17 C
17	12	7	5	18		19	23	19	5	13	13	24
15		19		12		15		13		13		17
16	18	21	21	20	21	18		17	2	12	13	13
16		23		15		19		21		16		21
	23	25	19	1		26	5	18	25	24	18	

A B C̸ D E F G H I J K L M N̸ O P Q R S T Ø V W X Y Z

1 N	2	3	4	5	6	7	8	9	10	11	12	13
14	15	16	17 C	18	19 U	20	21	22	23	24	25	26

44

3	20	26	20	7	1		16		26	20	13	1
9		20		26		5	21	20	19			8
20	21	4	13	14	1		15		1	12	14	13
4				25		4		24		14		14
6	26	14	25	25	9	14	4	6		2	24	4
		12				18		9		22		3
1	8	18	24	26	13		26	1	2	14	2	13
4 N		26		21		20				20		
10	14	1		22	14	2	18	1	9	9	1	22
1		2		1		18		26				24
9 L	21	2	16		20		9	24	6	23	20	12
24			20	15	21	13		22		21		1
18 P	26	24	17		11		15	1	6	6	1	22

A B C D E F G H I J K L̷ M N̷ O P̷ Q R S T U V W X Y Z

1	2	3	4 N	5	6	7	8	9 L	10	11	12	13
14	15	16	17	18 P	19	20	21	22	23	24	25	26

45

2	21	24	25	22	9	21	■	17	18	9 **D**	18	17 **M**
11	■	25	■	10	■	3	■	6	■	6	■	6
21	5	21	10	14	■	7	19	17	7	19	22	2
21	■	18	■	19	■	21	■	21	■	24	■	21
14	23	8	19	11	6	10	20	■	4	21	21	8
25	■	■	■	18	■	9	■	5	■	2	■	
26	19	20	22	8	14	■	13	6	10	21	2	14
■	■	25	■	9	■	19	■	8	■	■	■	23
1	19	19	16	■	19	1	2	14	18	24	25	21
18	■	1	■	17	■	21	■	22	■	19	■	18
2	12	22	21	18	16	26	■	19	8	1	6	14
6	■	25	■	15	■	21	■	22	■	8	■	8
2	11	21	9	21	■	9	21	2	24	18	25	21

A B C̸ D E F G H I J K L M̸ N O P Q R S T U V W X Y Z

1	2	3	4	5	6	7	8	9 **D**	10	11	12	13
14	15	16	17 **M**	18	19	20	21	22	23	24	25	26

46

18	23	10	1	19	25		15	13	14	1	23	16
23		8		26		22		6		24		26
21	6	18	14	23	26	8		10	2	26	14	8
18		24		3		18		26		16		6
15	2	10	1	26		22	1	20	20	1	2	14
13				15		22				23		2
	7	18	26	15	11		15	10	1	2	12	
10 P		10				5		6				24
26	2	14	6	15	6	8		15	1	12	8	2
9		1		1		2		13		6		23
6	14	16	26	23		2	8	5	6	17	2	12
18 U		11		16		10		6		15		2
13 T	2	13	11	2	14		2	4	13	2	23	12

A B C D E F G H I J K L M N O P̷ Q R S T̷ Ʉ V W X Y Z

1	2	3	4	5	6	7	8	9	10 P	11	12	13 T
14	15	16	17	18 U	19	20	21	22	23	24	25	26

47

8		4		5		3		2		3		11
6	24	21	8	23	25	22	18	14		24	14	24
24		24		16		25		21		16		16
4	19	4	25	3	23	25		24	15	10	4	16
26						24				8		14
24	7	23		5	23	21	21	22	18	22	12	
21		10		23				20		23		19
	8	2	23	17	4	17	4	14		25	22	16
8		8				23						22
12	23	1	1	4		24	16	24	1	24	25	2
10		4		12		18		20		9		13
18	10	21		5 **H**	23	10	8	24	17 **W**	22	18 **F**	24
18		2		24		16		21		2		3

A B C D E F̸ G H̸ I J K L M N O P Q R S T U V W̸ X Y Z

1	2	3	4	5 **H**	6	7	8	9	10	11	12	13
14	15	16	17 **W**	18 **F**	19	20	21	22	23	24	25	26

48

3	16	8	16	7	24		2	3	2	11	20	1
12		17		17				17		6		2
2	12	12		5	16	8	15	1	8	6	6	18
9		17		1		2		6				18
17	7	4	22		13	10	6	8	6	11	6	12
10		16		3		2		8		20		17
		1	8	17	10	7	7	17	1	1		
14		17		2		8		18		8		21
20	7	18	17	10 **R**	11	20	8		8	6	19	20
16				1		12		8		26		2
11	15	17	11	23 **K**	26	2	8	17		2	10	23
17		7		16				25		10		17
10	16	18	16	7	24		1	8	2	22	17	18

A B C D E F G H I J K̸ L M N O P Q R̸ S T U V W X Y Z

1	2	3	4	5	6	7	8	9	10 **R**	11	12	13
14	15	16	17	18	19	20	21	22	23 **K**	24	25	26

293

49

2	7	23	16	23	24		10	23	4	4	23	21
	26		24		23		8		9		1	
2	9	5	23	26	19	23	21		15	1	24	7
	12		1		8		7		23		24	
11	23	2	4		14	26	1	12	24	1	9	21
			17		26						26	
	25	14	23	2	4	9	8	26	9	26	20	
	14						24		26			
24	23	22	8	9	19 (C)	23	21		23	26	10	18
	5		14		8 (O)		23		13		1	
3	5	8	4		10 (V)	23	24	6	1	5	5	18
	23		21		23		23		19		14	
1	21	22	8	9	26		21	8	4	4	23	21

A B Ç D E F G H I J K L M N Ø P Q R S T U ¥ W X Y Z

1	2	3	4	5	6	7	8 O	9	10 V	11	12	13
14	15	16	17	18	19 C	20	21	22	23	24	25	26

	5		3		26		18		5		19
20	2	11	2	22	10		6	14	2	4	9	7
	13		8		11 **Y**		10		3		14	
10	12	22	7		5 **C**	2	5	17	9	19	9	8
	9				3 **H**		1		19		8	
9	16	6	10	26	9	19	6	12	9	7	
	12		3					13		10	
		19	9	21	22	1	10	1	12	1	2	13
	2		6		13		12			22	
2	14	9	19	12	22	19	9		10	1	8	8
	6		1		10		6		1		18	
25	19	2	13	15	9		23	6	24	13	22	23
	11		24		7		11		3		8	

A B ~~C~~ D E F G ~~H~~ I J K L M N O P Q R S T U V W X ~~Y~~ Z

1	2	3 **H**	4	5 **C**	6	7	8	9	10	11 **Y**	12	13
14	15	16	17	18	19	20	21	22	23	24	25	26

51

9	8	10	22	22		15	19	23	6	19 **A**	11 **K**	13
10		18		4		19		13		24		12
23	13	6	23	3	19	8		18	26	13	22	6
16		19		8				13				3
19	12	21	5	8	19	23		3	12	21	10	6
8		10				13		15		23		20
	3	12	2	5	3	22	3	6	3	10	12	
22		19		12		3				17		9
15	10	8	11	19		6	23	19	15	13	1	13
23				8				3		8		12
19	8	3	14	3		25	10	22	6	8	13	7
12		8		11		10		8		13		13
21	19	8	8	13	23	20		13	23	23	13	7

A̸ B C D E F G H I J K̸ L M N O P Q R S T U V W X Y Z

1	2	3	4	5	6	7	8	9	10	11 **K**	12	13
14	15	16	17	18	19 **A**	20	21	22	23	24	25	26

15		6	5	26	16		14	4	17	15		16
16	5	15			4		2			11	21	10
4		25		7	4	5	26(R)	24(U)		11		21
9	8	8	5		25		21		22	8	14	25
8		15		14	23	15	20	17		13		1
	23	26	14	23		10		21	20	8	15	
			10	8	15	25	23	8	5			
	14	25	17	8		15		10	17	11	13	
15		15		25	21	5	8	20		26		11
18	4	19	8		11		11		21	20	10	17
7		21		15	12	26	25	8		21		24
26	5	11			26		8			14	4	3
10		6	8	15	5		5	4	4	24		23

A B C D E F G H I J K L M̸ N O P Q R̸ S T U̸ V W X Y Z

1	2	3	4	5(R)	6	7	8	9	10	11	12	13
14	15	16	17	18	19	20	21	22	23	24(M)	25	26(U)

297

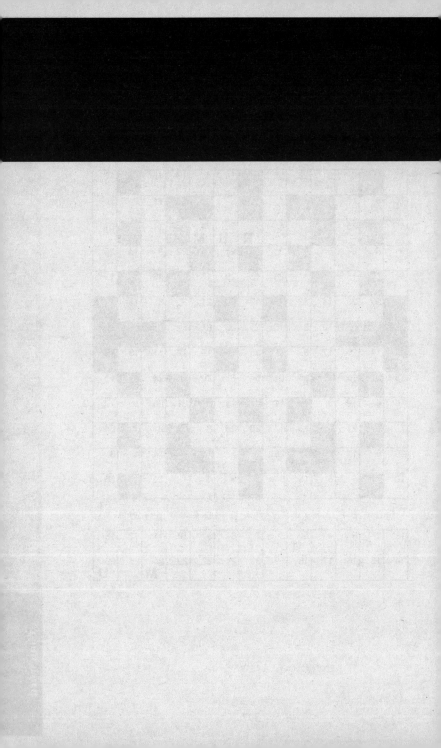

Solutions

Lexica
Solutions

Polygon
Solutions

Quintagram®
Solutions

Word Watch
Solutions

Codeword
Solutions

1

	K	N	E	L	T
	A				U
	Y		H	O	G
B	A	L	E		
	K		L		
			P	O	P

2

G				E	
R	A	B	I	D	
U		A		I	
M		L	O	T	
P	A	D		O	
Y			W	R	Y

3

C			D	O	N
H	A	M		A	
U		A	R	T	
R	E	D			
C					
H	A	I	K	U	

4

	F	I	N	D	
	A			U	
	C	A	D	E	T
	I		U		O
I	N	J	E	C	T
	G		L		E

5

	D			E	
	I	R	O	N	Y
	S			F	
C	A	R	R	O	T
	R			L	
	M	I	L	D	

6

			T	U	M
B	O	T	H		U
	V		R	A	M
K	A	L	E		
			A		
W	I	N	D	E	D

7

D	U	C	H	Y	
		R			
	S	A	B	L	E
B		F		O	
O	C	T	A	L	
G		Y		L	

8

F			S		
E	X	P	E	N	D
A			V		E
L	I	C	E		C
T			R		R
Y		S	E	X	Y

9

B		B	O	A	
E	M	U		P	
A		T	O	A	D
N	I	T		R	
	N			T	
	N				

10

S	T	I	L	E	
	H				
B	R	I	N	E	
	E		O		F
	S	P	O	K	E
	H		K		D

11

	S				
S	Q	U	I	R	T
	U			O	
T	I	D	A	L	
	S			E	
S	H	O	P		

12

	T		B		
	H	E	A	D	
	E		N		D
W	I	N	N	E	R
	R		E		E
		B	R	A	G

301

13

					M
	F	I	S	H	Y
	U		P		S
	R	E	A	C	T
		A			I
T	U	R	F		C

14

	F	A	C	E	T
	U		U		O
	G		T	U	M
D			T		E
R	I	C	E		
Y			R	U	N

15

	P		S		T
	R		N		H
F	E	L	I	N	E
	S		F		O
	S		F	I	R
			Y		Y

16

C	A	S	T	E	
O		E		G	
T	E	N	D	O	N
			I		E
	G	L	O	V	E
		E			D

17

		M		H	
G	O	A	T	E	E
O		I		A	
D	O	N	O	R	
				T	
	S	A	T	Y	R

18

T	A	B	B	Y	
	N		E		
	N	A	G		T
	U		O	R	E
V	A	I	N		A
	L		E	R	R

19

20

21

22

23

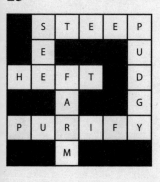

24

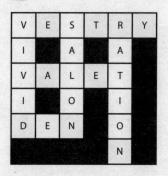

Lexica
Solutions

Polygon
Solutions

Quintagram®
Solutions

Word Watch
Solutions

Codeword
Solutions

25

					D
G	U	S	H	E	R
R		E			A
A		W	O	R	M
S	O	N		A	
S				G	

26

H			F		P
E	X	C	I	S	E
A			N		G
T	I	N	N	Y	
E			E		
R	O	O	D		

27

			C		C
	C	R	U	E	L
	O		L		U
L	O	A	T	H	E
	K			U	
		S	A	G	E

28

F	I	R	E		G
	S		R		R
P	O	T	A	T	O
	M				W
	E		A	R	E
A	R	C			R

29

A	L	L		P	
F		O	W	L	
T		V		E	
	F	E	U	D	
		R		G	
			V	E	T

30

B	O	D	E		
O					
B	E	L	U	G	A
C		O		N	
A		R		A	
T	W	E	E	T	

304

31

S	T	A	L	K	
	I		O		T
	R	O	U	G	H
	A		T		E
O	D	D			
	E				

32

	D	A	T	E	D
Z		I			
A	L	O	N	E	
P		K			A
		L	U	G	
	H	U	E		E

33

S		S		B	
C	H	I	L	L	Y
A		M		E	
N		I		S	
	P	A	N	S	Y
		N			

34

L	A	S	H		
	C		O		
	C		R		
I	R	O	N	I	C
	U		E		U
H	E	A	T	E	D

35

		P			
G		A			F
H	O	S	T	E	L
O		U			U
U	N	M	A	S	K
L					E

36

	M		J	A	R
T	I	L	E		A
	N		S	O	B
H	U	N	T		B
	T				I
M	E	W			

Lexica Solutions

Polygon Solutions

Quintagram® Solutions

Word Watch Solutions

Codeword Solutions

Lexica
Solutions

Polygon
Solutions

Quintagram®
Solutions

Word Watch
Solutions

Codeword
Solutions

37

		A	D	D
A	S	H		O	
	H		S	E	W
	E	Y	E		A
	E		L		N
	N	U	L	L	

38

	F		B	O	P
Y	O	G	I		E
	R		F	I	R
	U		O		I
E	M	B	R	Y	O
			M		D

39

	M	U	D		B
	I				U
	N	I	B		M
	D		A		P
		W	H	Y	
W	E	L	L		

40

A					
C	L	E	A	N	
E			L		K
	R	O	E		E
	U		R	I	P
B	E	L	T		T

41

F			O	L	D
U		W		O	
S	P	R	I	G	
E		Y		G	
			E	
	B	A	R	E

42

		F		M	
S	W	I	N	E	
I		L		N	
T		T			S
A	S	H	O	R	E
R		Y			T

43

W	R	I	G	H		T
A		C				R
F	E	Y				A
T			P			C
		F	E	A	T	
		P				

44

	B				C
J	E	E	P		A
	A		L	O	B
	R		U		A
V	E	R	M	I	N
	R		P		A

45

W	I	T			
A		O	R	B	
F	I	X		A	
E		I		D	
R	E	C	A	L	L
				Y	

46

S					F
L	I	M	E		L
A		O			A
B	E	D	P	A	N
		A		L	
B	E	L	I	E	

47

P	I	F	F	L	E
E			E		
A	S	K	E	W	
	E		T		
	E				
U	N	P	A	C	K

48

	S	U	L	L	Y
	O		I		A
	A		E	L	M
A	P	T		E	
T		I	M	A	M
E	K	E			

Lexica
Solutions

Polygon
Solutions

Quintagram®
Solutions

Word Watch
Solutions

Codeword
Solutions

49

B			C		
L	I	T	H	E	
A			E		
B	I	T	E		O
	C		P	I	P
	E				T

50

		D			
P	E	R	C	H	
		A		R		B
A	L	O	E			A
N				W	E	B
T	O	R				Y

51

F	L	O	O	Z	Y
	U			A	
D	R	Y		N	
	I		G	Y	M
	D	I	N		
			U		

52

A				U	
B	U	R	N	E	D
B			H		O
O		S	A	W	N
T			N		
	L	A	D	Y	

53

W	E	S	T		
		E			W
	V	A	L	V	E
	I		E		D
	C	A	N		
	E		T	O	P

54

		E			P
B	O	X			I
A		H	U	R	T
L		U		A	
M	E	M	O	I	R
Y		E		N	

308

55

		P			
C	O	A	L		F
H		R			O
I		S	A	F	E
N	E	E		I	
			E	N	D

56

H	A	T	P	I	N
	M		E		E
	E		R		W
E	N	S	U	E	
	D		S		
		P	E	C	K

57

S	P	A	C	E	
	L		I		T
B	U	N	G	I	I
	M		A	I	L
	B	A	R		D
					E

58

V	I	S	T	A	
A		O		D	
L	A	W		J	
U			W	O	N
E				I	
D	U	R	I	N	G

59

	P	U	B		
	R				D
C	O	S			A
U		L	I	L	Y
R		U		E	
B	I	G	O	T	

60

L	A	X			N
	X		S		A
H	E	L	M	E	T
A			A		T
L			C	O	Y
F	O	R	K		

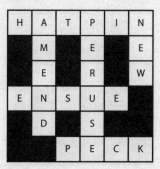
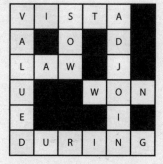

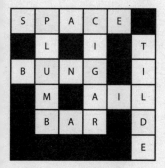

61

T	A	R	T	A	R
I			W		
C	O	B	A	L	T
K			N		A
			G		C
					K

62

P	E	A	H	E	N
O		I			U
S	A	D			B
I			P		
T	E	L	L		
			Y	E	W

63

R	U	S	K		
O		A		S	
D	O	M	I	N	O
E		E		O	
N			T	R	Y
T				E	

64

			O		T
B	E	A	V	E	R
E			U		I
D	O	O	M		V
		A			I
J	E	R	B	O	A

65

L			P		
O	C	C	U	R	
B			S		
B	A	S	H		
Y		I			
	S	N	O	U	T

66

	S		C		
	T	O	O		F
	A		M		E
	N	I	E	C	E
	C			A	
C	H	U	M	M	Y

310

Lexica Solutions

Polygon Solutions

Quintagram® Solutions

Word Watch Solutions

Codeword Solutions

67

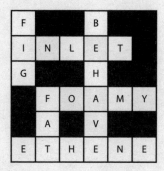

S	T	A	R	C	H
E				U	
L			G	E	L
F			U		O
		S	L	A	G
			F		

68

F			B		
I	N	L	E	T	
G			H		
	F	O	A	M	Y
	A		V		
E	T	H	E	N	E

69

B			V	I	M
R	I	S	E		A
A			X		N
I		I			L
L	A	R	K		Y
		K			

70

A	C	T			C
	E		A		A
D	A	N	G	E	R
	S		A		E
T	E	A	P	O	T
			E		

71

	A	L	L	E	Y
	R		O		A
	S	L	A	C	K
	O		F		
O	N		S	E	T
			R		

72

W	I	F	E		M
		A			A
	G	R	O	W	N
	O		A		U
C	O	R	K	E	R
	D				E

73

	J	E	W	E	L
	U		I		E
	M	I	N	C	E
	P			O	
				T	
L	E	T	T	E	R

74

S	H	I	F	T	Y
	A		I		E
	L		R		S
	L	U	M	P	
	O			A	
A	W	H	I	L	E

75

C	O	N			
U			P		
B	L	O	O	D	
	A		P		B
	N				O
	D	I	N	G	Y

76

H	A	G		V	
	S		L	E	G
	L			S	
S	E	X	I	S	T
	E			E	
	P	U	L	L	

77

S	H	I	F	T	
	O		A		
P	O	S	T		F
	P		A		A
		S	L	O	T
					E

78

W	I	C	K	E	T
	N				A
	F		J		K
A	L	L	U	D	E
	U		S		N
	X		T		

79

P	R	Y			
	E		G		
	A		R		P
F	R	E	E	Z	E
O			E		W
B	O	R	N		

80

T	E	N	N	I	S
A			A		T
R	E	B	U	K	E
			G		A
	T	H	U	D	
		T			Y

81

	B	U	R	S	T
	U		A		R
G	L	I	B		I
	L		B		A
		H	I	N	D
			T		

82

C	H	U	R	L	
O				Y	
O		F	E	L	T
P	I	E		I	
E			N		N
R		D	O	T	

83

E	A	R	W	I	G
		E			H
		P	I	K	E
Z	O	O			E
		S			
	W	E	E	D	Y

84

P	U	P			G
E		E			I
T	E	R	M		L
A			I	L	L
L	E	N	S		I
			T	E	E

313

85

A				D	
S	U	B	D	U	E
S		O		N	
U		A		K	
R	I	S	K		
E		T			

86

P	A	G	A	N	
	I		D		B
	S	H	O	N	E
	L		R		R
	E	R	E	C	T
					H

87

F	A	S	T		
L		N		F	
A		A		A	
S	K	I	N	N	Y
H		L		C	
				Y	

88

R		B			
E	Q	U	I	P	
F		L		U	
L	A	G	E	R	
U		E		S	
X			H	E	Y

89

T	A	U	T		J
Y					O
P	I	G			L
I		R	O	O	T
S		U			
T	A	B			

90

B			S		
I	C	I	L	Y	
R			O		S
D	O	U	B	L	E
	F				E
	F	R	I	S	K

314

91

	T	H	E	S	E
S		O		I	
M	O	G	U	L	
E				K	
A					
R	E	I	G	N	

92

S			P		
M	O	D	E		W
O			S		O
K	I	L	T		U
E			L		N
R		D	E	E	D

93

	T		F		
C	H	E	A	P	
	R		N		B
W	I	G			I
	C				L
B	E	A	G	L	E

94

			G	A	P
P	A	C	E		A
A			R	U	T
D	R	U	M		E
	A				N
	G	R	E	A	T

95

A	D	R	I	F	T
	O			E	
	D	O	Z	E	
	G			B	
	E	A	R	L	Y
			E		

96

B	A	L	M		
	K		A		S
	I	O	N	I	C
	M				A
	B				R
J	O	C	K	E	Y

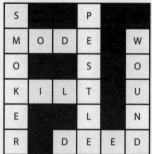

97

C	U	P	I	D		
		L				
	M	A	R	C	H	H
		I				A
G	I	N	G	E	R	R
						E

98

						H
		C	A	B		O
		H		O		L
S	I	N	G	L	E	E
I		U		A		
R	A	N	D	Y		

99

T	U	G			
A		L			T
B	O	A	T		E
O		N			N
O	L	D	E	S	T
					H

100

T		S			B
H	A	T	T	E	R
R		Y			A
O			K		Z
N		V	I	L	E
E			D		N

101

F					H
L	A	Z	E		U
A					R
W	O	M	B	A	T
E					L
D	O	G			E

102

D	R	I	E	S	T
	A			O	
	S			L	
S	P	I	D	E	R
	Y		U		A
		F	O	N	T

Lexica
Solutions

Polygon
Solutions

Quintagram®
Solutions

Word Watch
Solutions

Codeword
Solutions

103

	D		J		
D	I	V	I	D	E
	P		B		L
J	O	G			O
	L				P
	E	L	I	T	E

104

			D	I	G
P	A	L	E		U
A			W	A	S
S	A	W			H
T		O			
A	N	E	M	I	C

105

B	U	C	K		
U		U			
Z		B			B
Z	O	O	M		A
		I			R
	D	A	R	K	

106

C	H	E	A	T	
	I			R	
O	D	E		O	
			A	D	O
P	R	O	W		A
		E	L	F	

107

B	A	S	K	
O		H		P
W	H	A	L	E
		K		S
	D	E	A	T	H
		R		

108

		H	U	B
A	R	K			U
	I			R
G		L	U	G
F	I	N	E		L
	D		D	U	E

317

109

B	U	G			
E		I		Q	
L		R		U	
C	E	L	L	O	
H				T	
	C	L	E	A	R

110

	M				
B	U	D	D	Y	
	G		R		S
H		F	O	O	L
O			L		A
P	U	L	L	E	T

111

M	E	R	I	T	
A			N		
X		C	A	S	T
I			N		E
M	A	N	E		A
					K

112

		S		B	
D	E	T	A	I	N
		I		G	
T	O	N		W	
A		G	R	I	T
N	A	Y		G	

113

A					P
B	I	G			A
I			F		N
D	E	C	A	D	E
E			L		L
	H	O	L	D	

114

C	R	A	S	H	
	O		H		C
	T	H	E	T	A
W		E			N
A	I	R	M	A	N
D					Y

318

115

116

117

118

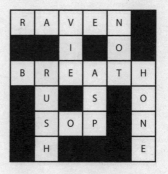

119

120

121

L	U	S	T		
	N				
C	H	A	P		C
	O		O		R
F	L	O	U	R	Y
	Y		R		

122

		S	A	N	G
T	A	P			U
I		O			N
M	A	K	E		N
I		E			E
D	U	N			R

123

	B	R	O	A	D
A		E			R
W	A	R	Y		Y
A		U			A
S	U	N	K		D
H					

124

K	O	H	L		
H		I			L
A	U	D	I	L	E
N		I			A
		N			S
M	A	G	N	E	T

125

S	N	E	A	K	Y
L				E	
I		S		Y	
V	O	L	E		
E		I			
R	U	M			

126

Z	A	P			
	T		B	A	D
	T		A		R
	U		T		A
U	N	H	O	O	K
	E		N		E

127

		F			K
M	A	R	E		I
A		U			D
Z		I			N
E	N	T	I	C	E
					Y

128

				P	
P	O	L	I	O	
A		U		L	
R	I	C	H	L	Y
R		I			
Y		D	O	V	E

129

B			U		
R	U	S	T	I	C
E			E		O
E			R		R
Z		J	U	N	K
E			S		

130

C	I	N	D	E	R
A			I		U
V	A	L	E		F
I		A			F
T	A	M	P		
Y		E			

131

	C	L	I	P	
	R			O	
S	U	C	K	E	R
	S			T	
C	H	E	E	R	Y
				Y	

132

	S	A	N	E	
	H			V	
B	A	C	K	E	R
	V		I		E
M	E	W	S		N
		S	O	D	

321

Lexica
Solutions

Polygon
Solutions

Quintagram®
Solutions

Word Watch
Solutions

Codeword
Solutions

133

	C		S		
	R	E	A	D	Y
	A		R		
	T	W	O		
	E		N		
F	R	I	G	I	D

134

	G		E	B	B
	O	W	N		E
	O		A		L
G	E	R	B	I	L
	Y		L		O
			E		W

135

F	L	A	T		
	E			C	
P	A	T	I	O	
	K			R	
				G	
C	R	I	T	I	C

136

S			W	I	T
H	U	G			A
A					R
P	R	E	S	E	T
E			A		A
D			P		N

137

					F
B	U	T	T	E	R
U		H			O
S	E	E	M		C
K		M			K
	G	E	T		

138

B				G	
A	B	S	U	R	D
N		C		A	
	L	O	I	N	
		L		G	
L	E	D	G	E	R

322

139

E	W	E			
G		N	I	L	
G	A	S		I	
		U	R	N	
		R		E	
	L	E	A	R	N

140

		R			S
D	A	I	S		W
A		D			A
B	L	E	A	R	Y
	A			A	
	G	R	A	N	T

141

C				
H	A	C	K	
E		H		
W	A	I	T		H
Y		V		A
	H	E	A	D	Y

142

E	N	C	O	R	E
	I				
	G	U	E	S	S
	G			E	
B	L	A	M	E	D
	E			D	

143

C	H	I	C	K	
	U		O		F
	L		I		L
	L	I	N	G	O
					W
	J	O	I	N	

144

	T		I	M	P
M	A	G		U	
	T			L	
S	T	I	L	L	
	O		Y		
V	O	Y	E	U	R

Lexica
Solutions

Polygon
Solutions

Quintagram®
Solutions

Word Watch
Solutions

Codeword
Solutions

1 course, courser, **coursework**, crus, cruse, cure, curer, curse, curser, cursor, cusk, ecru, euro, kouros, ours, recur, roué, rouse, rouser, ruck, ruse, rusk, scour, scourer, souk, sour, source, suck, sucker, sucre, suer, sure, user.

2 and, auld, dah, dal, dan, dhal, dual, fad, fah, fan, faun, flan, funda, fundal, half, hand, **handful**, haul, hula, lad, lah, land, laud, udal, uhlan, ulna.

3 bel, bell, blouse, blue, bole, boule, boulle, ell, leu, lobe, lobule, lose, louse, lube, lues, obelus, olé, ousel, sell, sleb, sloe, slue, sole, **soluble**, sue, use.

4 aegis, ageism, agism, amnesia, anise, gasman, gens, inseam, **magnesia**, manse, masa, mesa, saag, saga, sage, saiga, same, sane, sanga, seam, seaman, semi, siamang, sigma, sign, sine, sing, singe, snag, snig.

5 flour, **flourish**, flush, foul, four, furl, fusil, hilus, hour, houri, hurl, louis, lour, lush, ours, rush, shiur, shul, slur, soul, sour, surf.

6 bawd, braw, brew, dewar, draw, drawer, redraw, reward, tawer, wade, wader, wadi, wait, waiter, ward, warder, ware, wart, water, **waterbird**, wear, weir, weird, weta, wide, wire, wired, wirer, writ, write, writer.

7 enosis, ensile, eosin, illness, insole, isle, lenis, leonine, lesion, lien, lilo, line, linen, linn, lino, lion, lioness, lisle, loin, **loneliness**, niello, nine, noil, noise, nollie, noni, ollie, online, seine, seise, senile, sensei, sill, silo, sine, soil, sonsie.

8 err, ire, pep, per, peri, perp, pert, pet, pie, pier, pipe, piper, prep, rep, repp, ret, ripe, ripper, rite, tie, tier, tipper, tire, trier, tripe, **tripper**.

9 **acronym**, anomy, arm, army, cam, carom, coma, corm, cram, mac, macro, macron, man, manor, many, mar, marc, may, mayo, mayor, moa, moan, moray, morn, mornay, myna, norm, ram, roam, roman, yam.

10 erst, girt, girth, grist, grit, heir, hers, hire, irie, iris, reishi, resit, rest, right, rise, rishi, rite, shire, shirt, sighter, sire, stir, their, theirs, tier, tiger, **tigerish**, tire, trig.

11 elope, eloper, expel, explore, **explorer**, expo, leer, leper, lope, lore, orle, oxer, peel, peer, pele, père, plexor, pole, pore, prex, prole, reel, repel, repo, repro, role, rope.

12 abet, absent, **abstinent**, bait, bane, base, basin, basinet, bast, baste, bate, batiste, bats, batt, batten, bean, beast, beat, bent, best, beta, bias, bine, bint, bite, nibs, snib, stab, tabes, tabi.

Lexica
Solutions

Polygon
Solutions

Quintagram®
Solutions

Word Watch
Solutions

Codeword
Solutions

13 chill, choli, cholo, cill, clog, coil, color, cool, coolish, criollo, gill, girl, grill, hill, igloo, lilo, loch, loco, logic, logo, loris, olio, orchil, rill, roil, roll, school, **schoolgirl**, schorl, scroll, shill, shrill, sill, silo, slog, soil, solo, sool.

14 esse, est, ewe, née, ness, nest, net, new, news, newt, see, sen, sene, sense, sent, sente, set, sew, stew, sweet, tee, teen, ten, tense, twee, wee, ween, wen, west, wet, **wetness**.

15 ait, ant, anti, apt, inapt, ital, lat, lint, lit, nit, paint, pant, pat, pint, **pintail**, pit, pita, plaint, plait, plant, plat, pliant, tail, tan, tap, tian, tin, tip, tipi.

16 flesh, fleshy, floe, flor, flory, flyer, foley, herl, hole, holey, holy, **horsefly**, hosel, lore, lory, lose, loser, lyre, lyse, orle, rely, role, self, shelf, sley, sloe, sole, sorel.

17 cent, cento, cine, coin, conceit, cone, conic, conte, icon, into, nett, nice, nite, noetic, note, notice, once, ontic, **tectonic**, tein, tent, tine, tint, tone, tonic.

18 agio, bigha, biog, **biography**, bogy, brag, brig, garb, giro, gobi, goby, gora, gori, gorp, gory, grab, graph, grapy, gray, grip, gyro, orgy, pagri, pirog, porgy, prig, prog, yoga, yogh, yogi.

Lexica
Solutions

Polygon
Solutions

Quintagram®
Solutions

Word Watch
Solutions

Codeword
Solutions

19 cheder, cheer, cheers, cheese, churl, crush, desh, erhu, euchre, heder, heed, heel, herd, here, herl, hers, hurdle, hurl, lech, lecher, leech, lurch, lush, **reschedule**, ruche, ruched, rush, schedule, scheduler, shed, sheer, sherd, shred, shul, such, usher.

20 auk, aunt, auto, knout, koruna, kuna, kurta, nut, otaku, our, out, **outrank**, raku, rout, run, runt, rut, tau, tour, trunk, tun, tuna, turn, unto, urn.

21 aye, baggy, bay, **beggary**, bey, bray, bye, byre, eggy, eyra, gay, gey, gray, grey, gybe, gyre, raggy, ray, rye, yagé, yare, yea, year, yegg.

22 alevin, alien, anvil, eina, elan, lane, lean, levin, liane, lien, line, liven, lune, nail, naive, nave, navel, nival, ulna, **univalve**, unveil, vain, valine, vane, vein, venal, venial, vina, vine.

23 anna, anoa, anon, dang, dong, donga, **fandango**, fang, fango, fond, goanna, gonad, gonna, naan, nada, naga, nana, nonda, nong.

24 eerie, evil, exile, file, filer, fire, five, fiver, fixer, flier, ilex, lief, life, lifer, live, liver, refix, **reflexive**, reive, relief, relieve, relive, revile, riel, rife, rifle, rile, rive, veil, vile, vlei.

Lexica
Solutions

Polygon
Solutions

Quintagram®
Solutions

Word Watch
Solutions

Codeword
Solutions

25 citron, coir, contort, **contrition**, corn, croon, croton, crottin, inro, intro, introit, intron, intronic, iron, ironic, nitric, nitro, noir, nori, octroi, ricin, riot, ronin, root, roti, tiro, torc, toric, torii, toro, tort, tricot, trio, triton, tronc, trot.

26 eel, gee, gel, gelt, gen, gene, genet, gent, **genteel**, gentle, get, glee, gleet, glen, lee, leet, leg, let, née, neg, net, tee, teen, teg, ten, tenge.

27 act, aitch, cat, catch, cha, chai, **chaotic**, chat, chi, chic, chit, chota, ciao, coach, coat, coati, coca, cot, hic, itch, oca, och, otic, tach, tachi, tacho, taco, tic, tich.

28 alway, amyl, anomaly, anomy, away, lawny, layman, **laywoman**, loamy, manly, many, maya, mayo, moly, myna, noway, nyala, only, womanly, yawl, yawn, yowl.

29 aught, **daughter**, dearth, death, draught, earth, erhu, garth, gather, ghat, hade, hard, hare, hart, hate, hater, hatred, head, hear, heart, heat, herd, huge, hurt, rathe, rhea, ruth, tahr, thread, thru, thud, thug.

30 able, above, amble, ambo, bail, bale, balm, beam, bema, bile, biome, blame, boil, bole, boma, embalm, iamb, **immovable**, lamb, limb, limbo, lobe, mambo, mobe, mobile, movable, viable, vibe.

Lexica
Solutions

Polygon
Solutions

Quintagram®
Solutions

Word Watch
Solutions

Codeword
Solutions

31 desh, deshi, dish, fiendish, finish, finisher, fireship, fish, fisher, fresh, **friendship**, heir, herd, hers, hide, hider, hind, hinder, hire, hispid, nerdish, nesh, perish, pish, pisher, redfish, refinish, reishi, rishi, shed, shen, sherd, sherif, shin, shine, shiner, ship, shire, shred, shrine.

32 **contour**, cor, corn, cornu, court, croon, croton, crouton, cru, cur, curt, nor, orc, our, outro, roc, roo, root, rot, rout, run, runt, rut, tor, torc, toro, tour, tronc, turn, urn.

33 chit, cite, echt, etch, eth, ethic, hit, itch, ketch, kit, kite, kith, tec, tech, the, thick, **thicket**, tic, tich, tick, ticket, tie, tike, tit, titch, tithe.

34 **emission**, enosis, eosin, imine, ionise, issei, meiosis, meno, meson, mess, mien, mine, mossie, ness, nisei, noise, nome, nose, omen, seisin, semi, sine, some, sone, sonsie.

35 cent, cert, cruet, cure, cute, ecru, erupt, pent, pert, prune, puce, **puncture**, punter, pure, rent, rune, tern, truce, true, tune, tuner, untrue.

36 arch, arco, cargo, carom, carr, char, charm, charr, charro, chroma, coma, corf, corm, crag, cram, **frogmarch**, macho, macro, marc, march, mocha, morcha, orach, orca, roach.

Lexica
Solutions

Polygon
Solutions

Quintagram®
Solutions

Word Watch
Solutions

Codeword
Solutions

37 apex, axel, axil, axion, axle, axon, exalt, exit, exon, expat, expiation, explain, explant, exploit, expo, extol, ilex, ixia, latex, next, nixie, oxlip, oxtail, pixel, **pixelation**, pixie, pixilate, poleax, taxi, taxol, taxon, toxin.

38 age, ague, are, argue, auger, ear, emu, era, erg, game, gamer, gammer, gear, gem, gemma, germ, geum, gramme, mage, mare, marge, mega, murage, mure, rage, ream, reg, rem, rue, **rummage**, urea, urge.

39 erst, est, eth, her, hers, hest, hew, rest, ret, set, sett, sew, she, shew, shrew, stet, stew, strew, **strewth**, test, the, thew, tret, west, wet, whet, wrest.

40 **ablution**, about, abut, abutilon, aunt, auto, blunt, botulin, boult, bout, built, bunt, buntal, lout, lutino, tabu, tolu, tuba, tubal, tuna, ulna, unbolt, unit, unlit, until, unto.

41 acer, acre, caner, care, carer, carr, carry, cran, crane, cryer, earn, errancy, eyra, jerry, **jerrycan**, nacre, narc, nary, near, race, racer, racy, rare, rear, yare, yarn, year, yearn.

42 adept, adopt, adoptee, adoptive, atop, deep, depot, dopa, dope, epidote, epode, opiate, opiated, pate, patio, pave, peat, pied, pietà, pita, pivot, poet, tape, tepid, tope, topee, topi, vapid, veep, **videotape**.

Lexica
Solutions

Polygon
Solutions

Quintagram®
Solutions

Word Watch
Solutions

Codeword
Solutions

43 girn, grin, hint, insight, nigh, night, nights, **nightshirt**, nisi, ring, rising, shin, shirting, sign, sing, sitting, snig, snit, sting, stint, string, thin, thing, ting, tint, tithing.

44 abet, above, ave, bate, beat, bet, beta, bite, boatie, boîte, eat, eta, **obviate**, ovate, tea, tie, toe, toea, vet, veto, vibe, vie, voe, vote.

45 acer, acre, arame, arc, are, area, arm, camera, car, care, cram, cream, crema, ear, era, maar, macer, **macramé**, mar, marc, mare, race, ram, ream, rec, rem.

46 fight, filth, firth, flight, flirt, flit, fright, frit, fruit, gift, gilt, girt, girth, glut, grift, grit, guilt, hilt, hurt, lift, light, rift, right, **rightful**, ruth, thru, thug, trig, trug, turf.

47 code, coder, coir, cord, core, corvée, corvid, cove, coved, cover, credo, decor, devoice, devoir, devoré, divorce, **divorcee**, doer, dove, drove, erode, over, recode, redo, rode, rove, video, vireo, voice, voiced, voicer, void.

48 atom, homa, mahout, mash, mast, math, moat, mosh, most, moth, mouth, **mouthwash**, mush, muso, must, musth, sawm, sham, shawm, shmo, shtum, smut, soma, stoma, stum, sumo, wham, whom.

49 bice, bile, bine, blin, ceil, cine, civil, cline, evil, incline, **invincible**, levin, lien, line, linen, linn, live, liven, nice, nine, veil, vein, vibe, vice, vile, vincible, vine, vlei.

50 dour, drug, drum, dug, dum, dump, duo, gourd, group, grump, gum, **gumdrop**, gur, mud, mug, oud, our, pour, proud, pud, pug, roup, rug, rum, rump, ump, updo.

51 loo, loot, loss, lost, lot, loti, lots, oil, olio, silo, sloot, slot, soil, sol, solo, **soloist**, sool, soot, sot, sotol, stool, toil, too, tool, toss.

52 anti, aunt, intima, intuit, matt, mint, mitt, mutant, muti, mutt, taint, taunt, taut, tian, tint, titan, **titanium**, titi, tuna, unit.

53 bedel, behold, **beholden**, bleed, blend, blende, blond, blonde, bold, bole, dele, dhol, dhole, dole, heel, hold, hole, lend, leno, leone, lobe, lobed, lode, loden, lone, noble, olde, olden.

54 açai, alas, alias, also, ascus, asocial, assai, assail, cassia, casual, caul, causal, ciao, class, coal, cola, laic, lass, lassi, lasso, lias, oasis, sail, **salacious**, salsa, saola, sisal, soca, social, sola.

Lexica
Solutions

Polygon
Solutions

Quintagram®
Solutions

Word Watch
Solutions

Codeword
Solutions

55 fino, fogy, föhn, frog, giro, gonif, gori, gory, groin, gyro, gyron, hongi, horn, horny, horrify, **horrifying**, info, inro, iron, irony, noir, nori, orgy, origin, rhino, rigor, yogh, yogi, yogini, yoni.

56 clonus, clot, clou, clout, col, colt, consul, **consult**, cult, locus, locust, lost, lot, lots, lotus, lout, lust, slot, slut, sol, soul, tolu.

57 awe, ewe, ewer, haw, hew, hewer, raw, taw, tawer, thaw, thew, twee, war, ware, wart, wat, water, wear, **weather**, wee, wet, weta, wether, whare, what, wheat, whee, where, **whereat**, whet, wrath, wreath, **wreathe**.

58 aglow, allow, along, alow, ball, **ballgown**, ballon, bawl, blag, blog, blow, blown, boll, bowl, gall, gallon, gaol, glob, global, glow, goal, lawn, llano, loan, long, wall.

59 enter, enure, erne, fern, fetter, free, fret, neuter, nutter, reef, refute, rent, rete, retune, rune, runt, tenter, tenure, tern, terne, tree, treen, tret, true, tuner, tureen, turf, turn, **unfetter**, unfree, utter.

60 amiss, apse, apsis, impasse, **impassive**, mass, massé, massive, mavis, mesa, pass, passé, passim, passive, pave, same, samp, save, seam, sepia, spae, spam, spasm, vamp, vase, visa.

Lexica
Solutions

Polygon
Solutions

Quintagram® Solutions

Word Watch
Solutions

Codeword
Solutions

61 acne, anele, cane, caner, careen, clan, clean, cleaner, cran, crane, crenel, earn, earner, elan, enlace, erne, fane, fence, fencer, fern, flan, franc, freelance, **freelancer**, lance, lancer, lane, larcener, larn, lean, learn, learner, nacre, narc, near, ranee, relearn, renal.

62 act, cad, cap, capo, capot, cast, cat, coast, coat, cod, coda, cop, cos, cost, costa, cot, oca, octad, pact, **podcast**, sac, scad, scat, scot, soca, taco.

63 enjoy, eon, euro, jeon, joe, joey, **journey**, joy, nor, one, oner, ore, our, roe, rone, roué, yon, yore, you, your.

64 agist, alight, gait, gash, **gaslight**, gaslit, ghat, glia, haggis, hail, halt, ital, lash, last, lath, lathi, latish, lias, litas, sail, salt, sati, shag, slag, slat, stag, tail, tash, thali.

65 arco, calf, calk, call, carl, carol, cloak, coal, cola, collar, coral, corf, cork, croak, flack, floc, flock, focal, frock, lack, local, lock, orca, rack, rock, **rockfall**.

66 abeam, amass, amasser, amber, ameba, arame, barm, beam, bema, berm, bream, **embarrass**, maar, mare, masa, maser, mass, massé, mesa, mess, ream, rearm, samba, sambar, same, seam, smear.

67 bench, boho, chin, chine, chino, chip, chop, cohen, coho, cohoe, echo, epoch, hobo, hone, hoon, hoop, hope, inch, neophobic, niche, oche, ochone, ohone, phobic, phocine, phoenix, phon, phone, phonic, phono, pinch, poncho, pooch, pooh, **xenophobic**.

68 aim, animus, autism, ism, main, man, mantis, manus, mast, mat, matins, mint, minus, mist, mun, must, muti, nim, santim, sim, smut, stum, sum, tam, **tsunami**, tum.

69 able, alb, ale, all, aloe, bale, ball, bel, bell, bole, boll, ell, lab, label, lav, lave, lea, leal, lev, loa, lob, lobe, **lovable**, love, olé, oval, vale, veal, vole.

70 beedi, bend, betide, bide, bidet, bind, debit, debt, deed, dene, deni, dent, diene, diet, dine, dint, edit, endite, ident, **indebted**, indeed, need, nide, tend, tide, tied, tined.

71 alar, alarm, amah, arak, haar, haka, halal, hall, **hallmark**, halma, haram, hark, harm, kara, karma, kraal, lahar, lakh, lama, lark, llama, maar, maha, malar, mall, mark, marka, marl.

72 disown, down, dowt, drown, midtown, nowt, snow, stow, strow, swim, sword, sworn, swot, town, trow, twin, wind, **windstorm**, wino, wisdom, wont, word, worm, worn, wors, worst, wort, wrist, writ.

Lexica
Solutions

Polygon
Solutions

Quintagram®
Solutions

Word Watch
Solutions

Codeword
Solutions

73 acme, amerce, ampere, arame, came, camera, camp, camper, cram, cramp, cream, crema, creme, emcee, kame, karma, keema, kemp, maar, mace, macer, mack, make, maker, marc, mare, mark, marka, meek, mere, pacemaker, **peacemaker**, perm, pram, raceme, ramp, ream, remake, remap.

74 aid, ail, aim, amid, dais, dial, dim, dis, dismal, idli, ism, lias, lid, lis, maid, mail, mid, midi, mil, mild, **misdial**, said, sail, salmi, sild, sim, slim.

75 desk, **desktop**, despot, dose, est, estop, kes, peso, pest, pesto, pose, post, sept, set, sked, skep, sod, soke, sop, sot, spod, spoke, spot, step, stoep, stoke, stoked, stop, stope, tops.

76 afar, afraid, anuria, aria, arid, aura, darn, dinar, drain, durian, durn, fair, farad, farina, fraud, furan, nadir, naira, nard, radian, raid, rain, rand, rani, riad, rind, ruin, **unafraid**, unfair.

77 befit, belie, belief, bile, bill, billet, bite, elite, file, filet, fill, fillet, flit, leftie, libel, lief, life, **lifebelt**, lift, lilt, lite, tile, till.

78 append, dapper, dare, darn, dean, dear, denar, drape, espada, nada, napped, nard, nerd, padre, panda, pander, papad, parade, pard, rand, read, redan, rend, sand, sander, **sandpaper**, sard, sedan, send, spade, spend, spread.

79 cill, clonic, clou, coil, colic, colon, colonic, color, colour, cool, couloir, council, **councillor**, councilor, criollo, cull, curl, lilo, lino, lion, loco, loin, loon, lorn, lour, noil, null, olio, orcinol, rill, roil, roll, uncoil, uncool, unicolor, unrolls.

80 bee, beef, beet, befit, ben, **benefit**, bent, bet, bine, bite, eft, fee, feeb, feint, fen, fete, fie, fine, neb, née, net, nite, tee, teen, tein, ten, tie, tine.

81 ell, gel, ghoul, glue, gull, hell, hello, hole, hull, hullo, leg, leu, log, loge, lough, lug, luge, **lughole**, ogle, olé.

82 abort, about, abut, auto, bard, bardo, baud, boar, board, boart, boat, bora, brad, brat, broad, dart, daub, dobra, drab, drat, **outboard**, road, rota, rubato, taboo, tabor, tabu, taro, toad, trad, tuba.

83 **appraise**, apprise, aria, arise, aspire, pair, paisa, peri, pier, pipe, piper, praise, prise, raise, ripe, rise, sari, sepia, serai, sipe, sipper, sire, spiraea, spire, spirea.

84 erne, ever, evermore, meneer, mere, more, moreen, morn, mover, nerve, never, **nevermore**, norm, oner, ormer, over, reeve, remove, remover, revere, romer, rone, rove, rover, veer, veneer, vomer.

85 adios, dais, diss, dosa, doss, dust, fast, **fastidious**, fatso, fist, foist, fossa, fuss, oasis, oast, oust, sadist, said, sati, sift, soda, sofa, soft, softa, staid, stifado, stoa, stud, studio, suds, suit, tass, tosa, toss, ustad.

86 drupe, drupel, due, duel, dueler, dupe, duper, duple, elude, leu, lud, lur, lure, **prelude**, prude, pud, pul, pule, pure, purée, purl, rude, rue, rule, ruled, rupee.

87 aga, again, agin, ana, ani, any, gain, **gainsay**, gas, gay, nag, naga, nay, saag, sag, saga, saiga, san, sanga, say, saying, snag, yang.

88 berm, bier, biome, **biometry**, biro, bite, biter, boer, boîte, bore, bort, brim, brio, brome, byre, byte, embryo, mobe, mobey, obey, obit, obiter, ombre, orbit, robe, timber, timbre, tomb, tribe.

89 dole, dowel, less, lewd, lode, loess, loose, lose, loss, olde, sled, slew, sloe, slow, soldo, sole, solo, sool, weld, wels, wold, **woodless**, wool.

90 eerie, erne, inker, inner, **innkeeper**, keener, keeper, kern, kerne, nerine, nerk, peer, peerie, père, peri, perk, pier, piker, preen, prink, reek, rein, renin, repine, rink, ripe, ripen.

Lexica
Solutions

Polygon
Solutions

Quintagram®
Solutions

Word Watch
Solutions

Codeword
Solutions

91 acrylic, actuary, acuity, acyl, airy, alacrity, **articulacy**, arty, aryl, city, clarity, clarty, clary, clay, curacy, curly, lacy, lairy, laity, lyric, lytic, racy, riyal, talcy, tray, yaar, yatra, yuca, yucca, yurt.

92 know, knower, **network**, new, newt, now, nowt, owe, own, owner, owt, row, rowen, tow, tower, town, trow, two, twonk, wen, wet, woe, wok, won, wonk, wont, work, worn, wort, wren.

93 **elitist**, est, islet, its, lest, let, list, lit, lite, set, sett, silt, sit, site, slit, stet, stile, stilt, test, tie, tile, tilt, tit, titi, title.

94 aloe, arbor, arbour, boar, boer, bole, bora, bore, boreal, borer, boule, burro, euro, labor, laborer, labour, **labourer**, lobar, lobe, lore, lour, oral, orle, orra, roar, robe, role, rouble, roué, rubeola.

95 enlist, inlet, inset, lenis, lenity, lens, lentil, lien, line, lint, lintel, linty, liny, listen, lysin, lysine, nelly, nest, nite, sent, silent, sine, snit, stein, syne, tein, tine, tinsel, **tinselly**, tiny.

96 arak, asker, cake, cask, chakra, charka, crake, creak, hácek, hack, hacker, haka, hake, hark, **haversack**, heck, kara, kasha, kava, kesh, rack, rake, reck, sack, sake, saker, sark, shack, shake, shaker, shark.

Lexica
Solutions

Polygon
Solutions

Quintagram®
Solutions

Word Watch
Solutions

Codeword
Solutions

97 enquire, equid, equine, queen, queer, quern, queue, quid, quiet, quieten, quietude, quin, quint, quinte, quire, quirt, quit, quite, requite, tuque, unique, unquiet, **unrequited**.

98 alp, ape, gap, gape, gip, lap, lapel, leap, lip, lipa, page, pail, pal, pale, pall, pea, peal, peg, pia, pial, pie, pig, pile, pilea, pill, **pillage**, plage, plea, plié.

99 adman, ana, and, arm, dam, damar, damn, dan, darn, dram, drama, maar, mad, madras, man, mana, **mansard**, mar, masa, nada, nard, rad, ram, rand, sad, san, sand, sard.

100 **dilution**, diol, doit, dolt, donut, dout, idiot, idol, into, lido, lino, lion, loin, loti, loud, lout, ludo, lutino, noil, toil, tolu, udon, undo, unto, untold.

101 center, centre, cere, cert, cheer, chert, enter, erect, erne, etcher, ether, here, nether, recent, rent, renter, retch, rete, **retrench**, tenrec, terce, tern, terne, there, three, tree, treen, trench, **trencher**.

102 açai, acid, acidy, adda, addy, caddy, cadi, candid, candida, **candidacy**, candy, canid, cicada, cyan, cyanic, cycad, dada, dandy, dayan, diya, dyad, dyadic, nada, naiad.

103 bison, bonus, boss, bossism, bosun, buss, ibis, minibus, minus, miosis, miso, miss, mission, missis, missus, moss, muso, muss, nibs, nimbus, nisi, nous, omnibus, onus, sinus, snib, snob, snub, **submission**, sumo, suss.

104 chi, chic, chick, **chicken**, chin, chine, chink, cinch, cine, hic, hick, hie, hike, hin, ice, inch, ink, kin, nice, niche, nick.

105 air, airer, ait, **arbiter**, bait, barite, beira, bier, birr, bit, bite, biter, briar, brier, irate, ire, rai, **rarebit**, ria, rib, rite, tabi, terai, tie, tier, tire, tribe, trier.

106 dill, diol, doll, dolt, fill, filo, flit, flood, **floodlit**, foil, fold, folio, fool, idol, lido, lift, lilo, lilt, loft, loot, loti, olio, till, toil, toll, tool.

107 astute, quart, quarte, quartet, quest, rusa, ruse, rust, sauté, square, squat, squatt, **squatter**, statue, stature, strut, suer, suet, sura, sure, sutra, sutta, taut, true, trust, urate, urea, user, utter.

108 ding, dingo, diol, doing, dong, dung, dunlin, find, fluid, fold, folding, fond, found, **foundling**, fund, fundi, funding, fungoid, gild, gold, guidon, guild, idol, lido, loud, ludo, udon, undo, undoing, unfold.

109 cervix, civet, corvée, cove, cover, covert, covet, ever, evert, evict, evictor, excretive, over, **overexcite**, overt, receive, reeve, reive, revet, rive, rivet, rove, trove, vector, veer, vérité, vert, vertex, veto, vetoer, vexer, vice, victor, vireo, voice, voicer, vortex, vote, voter.

110 air, app, arak, aria, ark, kai, kappa, kara, pair, pap, papa, **paprika**, par, para, park, parka, parp, pia, pika, rai, raki, rap, ria.

111 aeon, alone, amen, anole, elan, eon, halon, hen, hon, hone, lane, lean, leman, lemon, leno, loan, lone, man, mane, **manhole**, mean, melon, meno, moan, name, nome, omen, one.

112 agio, arco, cargo, carious, ciao, coir, corgi, cougar, curio, giaour, giro, gora, gori, **gracious**, guiro, orca, oscar, ours, rugosa, sago, scoria, scour, soar, soca, sora, sour.

113 elver, ever, evolve, leer, lever, lore, love, lover, orle, over, reel, revel, revolve, **revolver**, role, rove, rover, veer, verve, vole.

114 cede, cedi, cine, deign, dene, deni, dice, diene, dine, edge, ending, engine, gene, genic, genie, iced, indene, indie, **indigence**, indigene, need, nene, nice, nide, niece, nine.

Lexica
Solutions

Polygon
Solutions

Quintagram®
Solutions

Word Watch
Solutions

Codeword
Solutions

115 bamboozle, **bamboozler**, bazoo, bazoom, bezoar, blaze, blazer, booze, boozer, bozo, braze, laze, maze, mazer, ooze, orzo, raze, rebozo, zeal, zebra, zero, zoom.

116 cent, cento, cite, **conceit**, conte, cot, cote, into, net, nit, nite, noetic, not, note, notice, ontic, otic, tec, tein, ten, tic, tie, tin, tine, toe, ton, tone, tonic.

117 heir, hep, her, hew, hie, hire, ire, pep, per, peri, perp, pew, phew, pie, pier, pipe, piper, prep, rep, repp, ripe, weir, **whipper**, wipe, wiper, wire.

118 **alacrity**, altar, artic, arty, atrial, carat, cart, citral, city, clarity, clart, clarty, ictal, ital, laity, lariat, latria, lytic, raita, rata, rictal, taal, tail, tala, talc, talcy, tiara, trail, tray, triac, trial, yatra.

119 elusion, **emulsion**, ileum, ileus, lieu, louis, louse, lues, lumen, lune, menu, minus, moue, moulin, mouse, muesli, mule, muon, muse, muslin, muso, neum, nous, oleum, onus, ousel, slue, slum, soul, sumo.

120 aware, bawl, beware, braw, brawl, brew, ewer, **tableware**, tawa, tawer, trawl, twee, wale, warble, ware, wart, water, weal, wear, wearable, weber, welt, welter, weta.

Lexica
Solutions

Polygon
Solutions

Quintagram®
Solutions

Word Watch
Solutions

Codeword
Solutions

121 adios, aphid, dais, danio, dash, dauphin, **dauphinois**, dipso, dish, dopa, dosa, dosh, dosha, dupion, hand, hind, hispid, hound, nidus, ophidian, poind, pond, pound, sadhu, said, sand, sandhi, sapid, shad, soda, sound, spod, spud, udon, undo, unipod, unpaid, unsaid, unshod, updo.

122 def, deft, defy, deify, deity, die, diet, dye, edgy, edify, edit, eft, fetid, fey, fidget, **fidgety**, fie, get, gey, gifted, gîte, ide, ted, teg, tide, tie, tied, yet, yeti.

123 arm, elm, lam, lame, lamer, lemma, male, malm, mam, mar, mare, marl, maser, meal, mela, mesa, ram, realm, ream, rem, same, seam, slam, **slammer**, smarm, smear.

124 adios, basin, bias, bison, bonsai, dais, dosa, ibis, naos, nibs, nisi, **obsidian**, said, sand, snib, snob, soba, soda.

125 cert, crest, cruet, crust, curst, curt, cute, **cutpurse**, erst, erupt, pert, pest, rectus, rest, rust, scut, scute, sect, sept, spurt, step, strep, stupe, suet, suture, truce, true, turps, upset, uterus.

126 emit, felt, file, filet, floe, item, left, **leitmotif**, lief, life, lime, lite, melt, metol, mile, mite, mole, mote, motel, motet, motile, motte, mottle, tile, time, title, toile, toilet, tome, tote, totem.

127 abed, able, abundance, alba, aubade, balance, balanced, bald, bale, banal, band, bandeau, bane, baud, bead, bean, beau, bend, blade, blanc, bland, blend, blue, bunce, bund, bundle, cabal, cable, club, cube, daub, daube, lube, nebula, unable, unbalance, **unbalanced**, unban, unbend.

128 arm, army, harm, **harmony**, hoar, hoary, hora, horn, horny, manor, mar, mayor, moray, morn, mornay, nary, nor, norm, oar, rah, ram, ray, rayon, rho, roam, roan, roman, yarn.

129 eon, inn, ion, leno, leone, **leonine**, lien, line, linen, linn, lino, lion, loin, lone, née, nene, neon, nil, nine, noil, none, noni, one, online.

130 hilus, hurl, lush, plus, plush, puli, pulp, pupil, puri, purl, **purplish**, push, rush, shiur, shul, sirup, slur, slurp, spur, uppish.

131 able, back, backlog, bagel, bake, bale, balk, beak, beck, black, blag, bleak, bloc, block, **blockage**, blog, bloke, boak, bocage, bock, bogle, boke, bole, cable, coble, gable, glob, globe, lobee.

132 mimsy, miso, miss, missy, mopy, moss, mossy, mousy, mumsy, muso, muss, mussy, myosis, opium, osmium, possum, simp, spumy, sumo, sump, **symposium**, yomp.

Lexica
Solutions

Polygon
Solutions

Quintagram®
Solutions

Word Watch
Solutions

Codeword
Solutions

133 envy, give, given, gyve, invite, naive, naivety, native, nativity, nave, navy, **negativity**, tantivy, vain, vane, vang, vanity, vegan, vein, veiny, vent, venti, viga, vina, vine, vintage, viny, vitiate, vitta.

134 ado, cad, card, chad, chador, chard, chord, cod, coda, cord, dah, dap, doh, dop, dopa, dorp, drop, hard, hoard, hod, pad, pard, **pochard**, pod, prod, rad, road, rod.

135 bel, belt, best, bet, blest, blot, boer, bole, **bolster**, bolt, bolter, bore, bort, bot, botel, bro, brose, lob, lobe, **lobster**, orb, rob, robe, sleb, slob, sob, sober, sorb, sorbet, stob, strobe.

136 amrit, anti, antrum, atrium, aunt, mart, martin, mint, muti, nutria, rant, **ruminant**, runt, rutin, tarn, tian, train, tram, trim, tuna, turn, unit.

137 beet, belt, beset, best, betel, blest, bole, bolete, bootee, botel, else, leet, lest, lobe, loose, lose, obese, oboe, **obsolete**, seel, sleb, sleet, sloe, sole, steel, stele, stole, telos.

138 ahimsa, amah, asthma, **asthmatic**, camas, cami, chasm, chiasma, maha, masa, mash, mast, mastic, matai, match, math, matt, mica, mist, mitch, mitt, scam, sham, shim, simcha, smith, tachism, tatami.

139 ennui, ileus, inner, insure, inure, isle, issue, issuer, lenis, lien, lieu, line, linen, liner, linn, nine, rein, renin, resin, riel, rile, rinse, rise, ruin, serin, sine, sinner, sinus, sire, siren, sunrise, **unruliness**, urine, ursine.

140 arak, are, area, ark, aye, ear, era, eyra, kaka, kara, kayak, **kayaker**, kea, rake, ray, yaar, yak, yakka, yarak, yare, yea, year.

141 deer, desire, dire, dree, druse, eider, ere, ire, red, rede, reed, reside, **residue**, reuse, rid, ride, rise, rude, rue, ruse, seer, sere, sir, sire, siree, suer, surd, sure, user.

142 agin, ailing, align, anti, atilt, gain, gait, giant, gilt, glia, glint, ital, ling, linga, lint, **litigant**, nail, nilgai, tail, tailing, taint, tian, tiling, tilt, ting, tint, titan, titi, titling.

143 chip, chirp, chiru, choir, cipher, ciré, coir, copier, curie, curio, epic, **euphoric**, heir, heroic, hire, houri, ichor, peri, pier, poui, price, puri, rice, rich, ripe.

144 alow, anew, bawl, bawn, below, blow, blown, bowel, bowl, elbow, fawn, flaw, flow, fowl, lawn, news, slaw, slew, slow, snow, swab, swale, swan, wale, wane, weal, wean, wels, wolf, **wolfsbane**.

1
1 Debut
2 Monet
3 Hidden
4 Manual
5 Red Admiral

2
1 Scam
2 Dallas
3 Crimson
4 Propose
5 Glossary

3
1 Quiz
2 Lemur
3 Lately
4 Cherish
5 John Milton

4
1 Thaw
2 Harsh
3 Psyche
4 Norfolk
5 Quadriceps

5
1 Chic
2 Mango
3 Joule
4 Persecute
5 Chieftain

6
1 Chile
2 Aloof
3 Jaguar
4 Stumped
5 Ted Hughes

7
1 Oust
2 Rhodes
3 Decapod
4 Fortune
5 Great tit

8
1 Bat
2 Liner
3 Modify
4 Jamboree
5 Greenhouse

9
1 Flock
2 Hardy
3 Poodle
4 Squeeze
5 Harmonica

10
1 Mare
2 Punt
3 Reset
4 Consensus
5 David Bowie

11
1 Pop
2 Iowa
3 Gimmick
4 Endanger
5 Don Bradman

12
1 Cast
2 Narrow
3 Antics
4 Incisor
5 Albatross

13
1 Jury
2 Rival
3 Trample
4 Scrawny
5 James Watt

14
1 Dial
2 Keen
3 Severn
4 Leapfrog
5 Anne Boleyn

15
1 Ghee
2 Drowsy
3 Exempt
4 Estonia
5 Affluence

16
1 Zoo
2 Nike
3 Britten
4 Prophecy
5 Invincible

17 1 Dairy
    2 Motto
    3 Choose
    4 Keswick
    5 Saxophone

18 1 Epic
    2 Claim
    3 Gibbon
    4 Mixture
    5 Jane Austen

19 1 Yak
    2 Plot
    3 Quiver
    4 Microchip
    5 Gastronome

20 1 Fidget
    2 Poland
    3 Mosque
    4 Tankard
    5 Dolphin

21 1 Fury
    2 Ounce
    3 Scallop
    4 Cluster
    5 Blindfold

22 1 Maze
    2 Hilt
    3 Plough
    4 Earl Grey
    5 Unorthodox

23 1 Dye
    2 Ghana
    3 Protein
    4 Imitate
    5 Binoculars

24 1 Pawn
    2 Tweak
    3 Sandal
    4 Hawthorn
    5 Harper Lee

25 1 Dour
    2 Genre
    3 Hobble
    4 Tendril
    5 South Downs

26 1 Ivy
    2 Craze
    3 Fanfare
    4 Legible
    5 The Tempest

27 1 Leap
    2 York
    3 Potent
    4 Asteroid
    5 Sauerkraut

28 1 Cab
    2 Stoat
    3 Pummel
    4 Test tube
    5 John Lennon

29 1 Onyx
    2 Frown
    3 Magnate
    4 Handsome
    5 Spitfire

30 1 Core
    2 Hyena
    3 Muddle
    4 Arduous
    5 Mumbo jumbo

31 1 Jinx
    2 Faced
    3 Squawk
    4 Apology
    5 Bar mitzvah

32 1 Mild
    2 Hoist
    3 Chorus
    4 Pioneer
    5 Anne Brontë

Lexica
Solutions

Polygon
Solutions

Quintagram®
Solutions

Word Watch
Solutions

Codeword
Solutions

Lexica
Solutions

Polygon
Solutions

Quintagram®
Solutions

Word Watch
Solutions

Codeword
Solutions

33
1 Deuce
2 Guard
3 Salver
4 Pontiff
5 Indonesia

34
1 Ban
2 Koala
3 Concise
4 Turmeric
5 Ferocious

35
1 Hat
2 Flax
3 Zodiac
4 Steel band
5 Alan Turing

36
1 Par
2 Grace
3 Physics
4 Death cap
5 Stockpile

37
1 D-Day
2 Nudge
3 Lodge
4 Cutty Sark
5 Bumper car

38
1 Pale
2 Kiosk
3 Galley
4 One-liner
5 On the ball

39
1 Gap
2 Mentor
3 Parish
4 Delicate
5 Rembrandt

40
1 Kayak
2 My Way
3 Shatter
4 Gremlin
5 Optimism

41
1 Folk
2 Grasp
3 Hazard
4 Apricot
5 Chelmsford

42
1 Safe
2 Mole
3 Joyful
4 Irrigate
5 Gerald Ford

43
1 Moot
2 Brute
3 Paradox
4 Obelisk
5 Commotion

44
1 Harp
2 Excel
3 Granite
4 Mollusc
5 Pink Floyd

45
1 Crime
2 Flair
3 Sherry
4 Quench
5 Gregarious

46
1 Tip
2 Bias
3 Geology
4 Ordinary
5 New Zealand

47
1 Poet
2 Grave
3 Riddle
4 Bluebell
5 Hot potato

48
1 Crave
2 Drift
3 Puffin
4 Hygiene
5 Mogadishu

Lexica
Solutions

Polygon
Solutions

Quintagram®
Solutions

Word Watch
Solutions

Codeword
Solutions

49 1 Foam
2 Muzzle
3 Parade
4 Samurai
5 Replenish

50 1 Mend
2 Conga
3 Dangle
4 Pharmacy
5 Sightseer

51 1 Sly
2 Overt
3 Swansea
4 Invoice
5 Marvin Gaye

52 1 Cork
2 Orion
3 Spanner
4 Bombard
5 Raspberry

53 1 Fun
2 Kerb
3 Larynx
4 Patriotic
5 Bleak House

54 1 Mayor
2 Speed
3 Polish
4 Limpet
5 Holy Island

55 1 Dip
2 Bodice
3 Neutral
4 Jubilee
5 Garibaldi

56 1 Bob
2 Crèche
3 Discus
4 Mastodon
5 Exquisite

57 1 Quit
2 Pecan
3 Frenzy
4 Foliage
5 Enid Blyton

58 1 Honey
2 Midas
3 Parka
4 Liberate
5 Goldfinch

59 1 Nod
2 Copper
3 Pontoon
4 Kalahari
5 One by one

60 1 Pond
2 Slap
3 Toddler
4 Frigate
5 Wordsworth

61 1 Judo
2 Spoof
3 Rostrum
4 Pageant
5 Interpret

62 1 Noon
2 Sharp
3 Haggle
4 Electron
5 Cleopatra

63 1 Fly
2 Glare
3 Mercury
4 Teetotal
5 Threshold

64 1 Cue
2 Stall
3 Gallant
4 Jeopardy
5 Succulent

65 1 Fair
2 Safari
3 Tariff
4 Ratafia
5 Satirists

66 1 Wary
2 Knee
3 Pierrot
4 Victoria
5 Selection

67 1 Drab
2 Squeal
3 Feigned
4 Remains
5 Downward

68 1 Group
2 Flower
3 Pickle
4 Justice
5 Question

69 1 Bus
2 Chump
3 Excerpt
4 Deranged
5 Recreated

70 1 Pip
2 Hive
3 Sticker
4 Tashkent
5 Cantaloupe

71 1 Soft
2 Credo
3 Thirty
4 Daughter
5 Constable

72 1 Pit
2 Topaz
3 Sexist
4 Prosecute
5 Starboard

73 1 Axle
2 Daze
3 Equip
4 Judgement
5 Babysitter

74 1 Green
2 Right
3 Spread
4 Dominant
5 Essayist

75 1 Cut
2 Truck
3 Rumpus
4 Buttercup
5 Pasternak

76 1 Wage
2 Byline
3 Threat
4 Jackpot
5 Greatness

77 1 Grace
2 Stand
3 Puffin
4 Streamer
5 Vinegary

78 1 Hymn
2 Odds
3 Aitch
4 Lubricate
5 Crustiness

79 1 Yeti
2 Serge
3 Rubens
4 Anagram
5 Reasonable

80 1 Bade
2 Minx
3 Senator
4 Wrapper
5 Mountebank

Lexica
Solutions

Polygon
Solutions

Quintagram®
Solutions

Word Watch
Solutions

Codeword
Solutions

81 1 Quit
2 Taxes
3 Justin
4 Tumbled
5 Smattering

82 1 Egad
2 Taxi
3 Lathe
4 Proscribe
5 Telepathic

83 1 Add
2 Vivid
3 Course
4 Quixotic
5 Hitchhiker

84 1 Hand
2 Elite
3 Counter
4 Supreme
5 Spotlight

85 1 Pad
2 Botox
3 Stripe
4 Volcanic
5 Conviction

86 1 Pelt
2 Eland
3 Indigo
4 Prospero
5 Stage door

87 1 Mason
2 Whine
3 Ragmen
4 Abandon
5 Brokerage

88 1 Mask
2 Trace
3 Leisure
4 Frighten
5 Parterre

89 1 Bear
2 Pence
3 Doublet
4 Crusades
5 Pullover

90 1 Dog
2 Goya
3 Night owl
4 Stallion
5 Slaughter

91 1 Nile
2 Figure
3 Legend
4 Measured
5 Palimony

92 1 Wash
2 Like
3 Litotes
4 Sustain
5 Integrally

93 1 Strut
2 Trust
3 Deadly
4 Stormy
5 March hares

94 1 Apex
2 Biting
3 Emails
4 Bequest
5 Dispersal

95 1 Pukka
2 Yukon
3 Monitor
4 Zebedee
5 Parallax

96 1 Kink
2 Coffer
3 Traipse
4 Twitter
5 Flounder

97 1 Clan
2 Spud
3 America
4 Galleon
5 Zabaglione

98 1 Maid
2 Close
3 Safest
4 Pageants
5 Flagstaff

99 1 Joint
2 Texan
3 Ragout
4 Furlong
5 Legendary

100 1 Arson
2 Basque
3 Jostle
4 Juniper
5 Kalahari

101 1 Pug
2 Eyot
3 Stair
4 Put forward
5 Vermicelli

102 1 Drop
2 Avoid
3 Vetoed
4 Rehoboam
5 Testament

103 1 Troy
2 Beast
3 Tagine
4 Tangier
5 Federalist

104 1 Ill
2 Quiet
3 Medical
4 Impaler
5 Grub Street

105 1 Apron
2 Actors
3 Primer
4 Postbox
5 Contents

106 1 Sumo
2 Canine
3 Emigre
4 Dream up
5 Antipasto

107 1 Tax
2 Just
3 Saintly
4 Chariest
5 Discipline

108 1 Mango
2 Ozone
3 Defect
4 Iberian
5 Ankle-deep

109 1 Cap
2 Queue
3 Stalag
4 Mistrust
5 Apparently

110 1 Ambit
2 Award
3 Baton
4 Passable
5 Flautists

111 1 Born
2 Feed
3 Yellow
4 Astronomy
5 Backfired

112 1 Raja
2 Equip
3 Squire
4 Downcast
5 Portrayal

Lexica
Solutions

Polygon
Solutions

Quintagram®
Solutions

Word Watch
Solutions

Codeword
Solutions

113 1 Zloty
2 Wizard
3 Zither
4 Bezique
5 Matchbox

114 1 Rear
2 Auction
3 Opening
4 Restful
5 Segment

115 1 Chat
2 Credo
3 Exmoor
4 Brigade
5 Saturnalia

116 1 Opal
2 Plane
3 Kingpin
4 Sketchy
5 Freelance

117 1 Argon
2 Flinch
3 Profit
4 Commons
5 Drowning

118 1 Fly
2 Hadj
3 Caravan
4 Pygmalion
5 Whetstone

119 1 Goon
2 Stray
3 Dozen
4 Quatrain
5 Ragamuffin

120 1 Aga
2 Askew
3 Hammer
4 Escapism
5 Minute hand

121 1 Know
2 Oral
3 Novel
4 Eliminate
5 Prospectus

122 1 Box
2 Stark
3 Shadow
4 Impounds
5 Marginally

123 1 Limo
2 Vicar
3 Groovy
4 Jaundice
5 Pas de deux

124 1 Hymn
2 Bright
3 Rumpus
4 Bananas
5 Stockroom

125 1 Isle
2 Muggins
3 Miranda
4 Rosebud
5 Enteral

126 1 Pawn
2 Houri
3 Jumper
4 Glazier
5 Cheapskate

127 1 Part
2 Clan
3 Atrophy
4 Deputise
5 Union Jack

128 1 Stay
2 Lodge
3 Sleepy
4 Triplet
5 Successive

Lexica
Solutions

Polygon
Solutions

Quintagram®
Solutions

Word Watch
Solutions

Codeword
Solutions

1 **TALLAGE** (b) A toll levied by a lord upon his tenants or by a feudal lord upon his vassals.

2 **JOINTURE** (b) The provision made by a husband for his spouse by settling property on her at marriage for use after the husband's death.

3 **BELLETRIST** (b) A fine writer or writer of belles-lettres.

4 **SPIRACLE** (c) A small aperture for allowing air to enter the body of insects or fish or the blowhole of a whale.

5 **AMENT** (a) Another name for a catkin. Also called amentum.

6 **TMESIS** (a) The interpolation of a word or group of words between parts of a compound word, eg ha-blooming-ha.

7 **INSET** (b)An inset day (IN-SErvice Training day) is one of five days in schools during term time on which school sessions are not run, and pupils do not attend.

Lexica
Solutions

Polygon
Solutions

Quintagram®
Solutions

Word Watch
Solutions

Codeword
Solutions

8   **OBELION** (c) An area of the skull where the sagittal
    suture meets the parietal foramina.

9   **QUILLET** (a) A quibble, a subtle argument.

10 **REPUNIT** (a) A number with the digits repeated,
    eg 11, 222, 3,333.

11 **SERVITE** (c) A member of the Order of Servants of the
    Virgin, founded in the 13th century.

12 **TECKEL** (b) A dog, another name for a dachshund.

13 **PAVID** (b) Fearful, timid, from Latin pavere to tremble.

14 **APAGOGE** (c) An indirect argument which proves
    something by showing the contrary to be absurd or
    impossible.

15 **GOBANG** (a) A Japanese board-game.

Lexica
Solutions

Polygon
Solutions

Quintagram®
Solutions

Word Watch
Solutions

Codeword
Solutions

16 **CATAPAN** (c) A provincial governor in the Byzantine Empire."

17 **TOCOPHEROL** (a) Vitamin E, found in wheat-germ oil, watercress, lettuce, egg yolk, etc.

18 **GLUME** (b) The outer bract of grass or sedge.

19 **NACKET** (c) A light snack lunch.

20 **STEEVE** (b) To incline a bowsprit upwards at an angle from the horizontal.

21 **KENSPECKLE** (b) Conspicuous, easily recognisable (Scots).

22 **LAPIDOSE** (b) Of a stony nature.

23 **MARCID** (a) Withered, wasted away, decayed, from Latin marcidus (see Mervyn Peake, Gormenghast).

Lexica
Solutions

Polygon
Solutions

Quintagram®
Solutions

Word Watch
Solutions

Codeword
Solutions

24 NESTLECOCK (c) The weakling of the brood, a runt.

25 VERDIN (b) A bird, a north American yellow-headed tit.

26 SELD (a) Rare, uncommon, adjectival form of "seldom".

27 MORSE (c) A walrus, from the Lapp morsa.

28 AVESTAN (c) The language of the Zoroastrian scriptures.

29 POGGY (c) A small whale.

30 MEW (a) A secret place or den.

31 SWEEPAGE (b) The crop of hay mown from a meadow.

32 ESURIENT (b) Greedy, avaricious.

Lexica
Solutions

Polygon
Solutions

Quintagram®
Solutions

Word Watch
Solutions

Codeword
Solutions

33 **VERTIBLE** (a) Inconstant, able to be turned.

34 **SEPTICAL** (b) Obsolete form of septic, producing putrefaction.

35 **HETHING** (a) Derision or scorn, from Old Norse hathung ("scorn, shame, disgrace").

36 **WEAL** (c) Wealth, riches, wellbeing.

37 **BAILOR** (a) Someone who retains ownership of goods but entrusts them to another under a bailment.

38 **BEVOR** (c) Armour that protects the lower part of the face.

39 **BELAR** (a) An Australian tree used for timber.

40 **BEGAR** (b) In India, enforced or compulsory labour, usually without payment.

41 KABADDI (b) An Asian form of the game of tag or catch.

42 ZITI (b) A type of macaroni.

43 FAGOTTO (a) An archaic name for a bassoon.

44 VENTURI (c) A tube used to measure the flow of liquids.

45 SOAM (b) A chain attaching a horse to a plough.

46 SHAB (b) Scab, an itching disease of animals.

47 LEISTER (a) A salmon spear.

48 DALLOP (a) A shapeless lump, a dollop.

49 DEGOMBLE (a) To clear snow off clothes, boots and so on (coined by Antarctic expeditions).

Lexica
Solutions

Polygon
Solutions

Quintagram®
Solutions

Word Watch
Solutions

Codeword
Solutions

50 SNITTERING (c) The soft, light fall of snow.

51 FEEFLE (a) To swirl, as of snow around a corner (Scots).

52 HOGAMADOG (b) A huge ball made by boys rolling snow (Northumberland).

53 SNIT (c) A fit of temper (US & Australian).

54 TONDO (b) A circular easel painting or relief carving, from Italian rotondo.

55 SALLET (a) A light helmet extending over the back of the neck; it replaced the basinet in the 15th century.

56 BUTTYMAN (c) A contractor who pays other miners to extract coal from a pit.

57 TROVER (c) The act of wrongfully assuming proprietary rights goods or property belonging to another.

58 CHOWRI (b) A fly-whisk made from the tail of the yak.

59 BASENJI (a) A small smooth-haired dog of African origin having an inability to bark.

60 BICHIR (a) An African freshwater fish with an elongated body.

61 MAESTOSO (b) As a musical direction, to be performed majestically.

62 WHERRY (c) A light rowing boat used in inland waters and harbours.

63 SARABANDE (a) A decorous 17th-century courtly dance.

64 FRENUM (b) A fold of membrane or skin, such as that beneath the tongue, that supports an organ.

65 THEORBO (c) An obsolete form of lute, with two necks, the second carrying a set of bass strings.

Lexica
Solutions

Polygon
Solutions

Quintagram®
Solutions

Word Watch
Solutions

Codeword
Solutions

Lexica
Solutions

Polygon
Solutions

Quintagram®
Solutions

Word Watch
Solutions

Codeword
Solutions

66 THEREMIN (a) An electronic musical instrument, named after Leon Theremin (1896-1993) and played by moving the hands through electromagnetic fields.

67 DITHYRAMB (b) A frenzied choral hymn, sung in honour of Dionysus.

68 AUSTRALORP (a) A chicken (contraction of Australian Orpington).

69 LEMMA (a) Part of an argument, a subsidiary proposition, used in the proof of another.

70 LENTICULAR (b) Shaped like a biconvex lens.

71 POILU (c) An infantryman in the French Army, especially one from the First World War.

72 REJONEADOR (b) A bullfighter who rides on horseback and spears the bull with lances.

73 WAYZGOOSE (a) A works outing made annually by a printing house, traditionally on Maundy Thursday.

74 SNAKEHEAD (a) On American railways, a metal spike used to secure the rails which could spring loose and penetrate the carriage with lethal consequences.

75 LEAGUER (c) A liquid measure, a barrel of a certain size, containing wine, oil or fresh water on a ship (Dutch).

76 GECK (c) (Scottish) an object of derision; a fool.

77 EUTHERIAN (a) Belonging to the Eutheria, a subclass of mammals that have a placenta and reach an advanced state of development before birth.

78 MONODY (b) In Greek tragedy, an ode sung by a single actor.

79 ABERGLAUBE (c) Superstition (from the German).

80 PERISELENIUM (b) The closest point of the orbit of a spacecraft to the Moon.

81 KNOP (a) An ornamental knob, especially on the stem of a chalice.

Lexica
Solutions

Polygon
Solutions

Quintagram®
Solutions

Word Watch
Solutions

Codeword
Solutions

Lexica
Solutions

Polygon
Solutions

Quintagram®
Solutions

Word Watch
Solutions

Codeword
Solutions

82 PLANISHED (b) Of metal, given a final finish by hammering.

83 EUTHENICS (a) Study of the control of the environment, with a view to improving health and living standards.

84 PALANQUIN (c) A covered Oriental litter carried on the shoulders of four men.

85 STONE (b) A table with a flat iron or stone surface on which printers compose hot-metal pages.

86 PIGHTLE (a) A small enclosure; paddock (Eastern England, archaic dialect).

87 EMMER (a) A variety of wheat thought to be an ancestor of many other types.

88 RAMSTAM (b) Headlong, hastily (Scots).

89 FALCONET (b) A cannon or field gun that fired a shot the weight of one falcon.

90 ALIZARIN (a) Red dye made from the madder root.

91 ROWEL The small spiked wheel attached to a spur.

92 SLEEVEEN (b) (Irish) A sly, obsequious, smooth-tongued person.

93 ALEPH (a) The first letter of the Hebrew alphabet.

94 KANJI (a) Chinese letters subsumed into Japanese writing."

95 ANABIOSIS (c) Returning to life after apparent death.

96 VORANT (a) Of a heraldic beast, devouring.

Lexica
Solutions

Polygon
Solutions

Quintagram®
Solutions

Word Watch
Solutions

Codeword
Solutions

Lexica
Solutions

Polygon
Solutions

Quintagram®
Solutions

Word Watch
Solutions

Codeword
Solutions

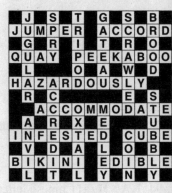

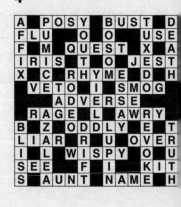

1

```
S T Y M I E   O C C U P Y
  H   I   N   R   A   R
L O P S I D E D   R U I N
  R   F   E   E   G   M
A N T I   M A R J O R A M
  R   I       R       R
  I N E X C U S A B L Y
  N       E   I
S Q U E E Z E D   L O B E
  U   A   E   U   L   E
V E S T   B E C K O N E D
  S   E   R   E   W   C
S T A N Z A   R H Y T H M
```

2

```
  J   S   T   G   S   B
J U M P E R   A C C O R D
  G   R   I   T   R   O
Q U A Y   P E E K A B O O
  L       O   A   W   D
H A Z A R D O U S L Y
  R   C           E   S
    A C C O M M O D A T E
  A   R   X   E       U
I N F E S T E D   C U B E
  V   D   A   L   O   B
B I K I N I   E D I B L E
  L   T   L   Y   N   Y
```

3

```
S P A S M   E A G E R L Y
  H   L   I   N   O U   E
R E L A X E D   R U M B A
  I   O   E       I   R
L O W E R E D   L I B E L
  L   A   R   L   U   Y
  I N E Q U I T A B L Y
F   C   U   E   L   A
A R E N A   D I V I D E D
S   C       O   O   M
T H A N K   J A C U Z Z I
E   D   E   A   A   E R
R E O R D E R   L A R G E
```

4

```
A   P O S Y   B U S T   D
F L U   O   O     U S E
F   M   Q U E S T   X   A
I R I S   T   O   J E S T
X   C   R H Y M E   D   H
  V E T O   I   S M O G
    A D V E R S E
  R A G E   L   A W R Y
B   Z   O D D L Y   E   T
L I A R   R   U   O V E R
I   L   W I S P Y   O   U
S E E   F   I     K I T
S   A U N T   N A M E   H
```

Lexica
Solutions

Polygon
Solutions

Quintagram®
Solutions

Word Watch
Solutions

Codeword
Solutions

5

```
A C U M E N   C U F F E D
O   O   E   R   O   F
E L O N G A T E   C A F E
L   S   R   E   U   E
J O L T   E X P O S U R E
Q   E   S         V
T U R R E T   S W A Y E D
I         E   M   S
P A I N T B O X   A R C H
L   I   U   T   Z   E
K I N G   G R A D I E N T
S   H   G   N   N   C
S M I T H Y   T U G G E D
```

6

```
C Y N I C I S M   T R E E
I   O   E   P   L   E   X
T A X E D   R O O F T O P
E   I   E   I   G   R   U
D O O M   S T U B B O R N
U   V   E   O       G
J E S T E R   M O U S S E
A     E   A   K   Q
C H E E R I L Y   T U N A
K   R   I   K   T   A   P
P I R A N H A   U N L E T
O   O   G   L   B   I   L
T A R N   W I Z A R D R Y
```

7

```
  A   S K S   C   J
E X P O N E N T   O B O E
L   N   R   I   N   Y
D E T A I N   R A V I S H
    T   E       E   T
A S S A U L T   C Y N I C
T       S   W       C
P R I Z E   F I N I C K Y
U   E       S   D
A G H A S T   T R E M O R
G   L   S   F   A   W
A L T O   A Q U I L I N E
E   T   R   L   S   S
```

8

```
  S C U L L   M O C H A
B   O   O   G   W   E   I
E R R   B R A W L   N U N
A   G       L       N   S
C H I C   P A T   G A I T
H     R A Y   E M U   I
C O L A   L   P   I R O N
O     Z O O   I L L   C
M A N Y   N O D   T E X T
B   O           E   I
E A T   S Q U A D   R E V
R   C   I   S   U   I   E
  W H A R F   J O K E D
```

369

9

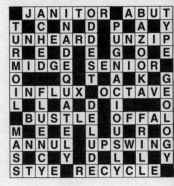

```
J U N I O R S   C R E E L
A   O   U   A   R X   U
C L O U T   S H A M A N S
K   K   B   H   W   C   T
D I S Q U I E T   S T A Y
A     R   S   F   L
W I S E S T   L A W Y E R
  N   T   B   U   E
B O O N   L O L L I P O P
E   O   L   U   T   R
F I Z Z I N G   I M A G O
O   E   D   H   E   V
G U S T O   S Y R I N G E
```

10

```
  J A N I T O R   A B U T
T   C   N   D   P   A   Y
U N H E A R D   U N Z I P
R   E   D   E   G   O   E
M I D G E   S E N I O R
O     Q   T   A   K   G
I N F L U X   O C T A V E
L   L   A   D   I     O
  B U S T L E   O F F A L
M   E   E   L   U   R   O
A N N U L   U P S W I N G
S   C   Y   D   L   L   Y
S T Y E   R E C Y C L E
```

11

```
E A R T H Y   W I Z A R D
Q   O   E     N   B   U
U P G R A D E   F L E C K
A   U   R   U   E   T   E
T W E E T   R A R I T Y
E   E   E   O     E
D I V I N G   F E U D A L
  I   J   X     O
  S C Y T H E   H Y E N A
O   T   A   E   U   N   T
P R O W L   R E M A T C H
U   R   O   E   E   E
S P Y I N G   A D O R E D
```

12

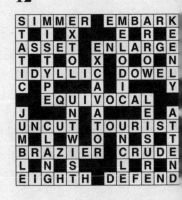

```
S I M M E R   E M B A R K
T   I   X     E   R   E
A S S E T   E N L A R G E
T   T   O   X   O   O   N
I D Y L L I C   D O W E L
C   P   A   I   Y
  E Q U I V O C A L
J   N   A     E   A
U N C U T   T O U R I S T
M   L W   O   N   S   T
B R A Z I E R   C R U D E
L   N   S   L   R   N
E I G H T H   D E F E N D
```

370

13

```
M O I S T _ R O A S T _ J
_ D _ I C E _ U _ H O E _
V E R G E _ B O X E R _ R
I _ E _ U _ I _ O _ _ K _
S T R E S S F U L _ B A Y
T _ U _ U _ F _ I _ I _ I
A W N I N G _ G A Z U M P
H _ _ S _ K _ R _ V _ _ I
S O B _ C A N D Y T U F T
Q _ R _ R _ R _ O _ L _ H
U _ A G E N T _ O V A R Y
A S S _ E _ T O R _ _ A _
T _ S A N D Y _ B I N G O
```

14

```
B U Z Z A R D S _ A B L E
O _ I _ C _ I _ S _ A _ X
O F T E N _ S T Y P T I C
M _ H _ E _ O _ M _ O _ E
S H E D _ T W O P E N C E
_ _ R _ D _ N _ T _ _ _ D
K I S S E S _ C O S M O S
I _ _ M _ M _ M _ A _ _ _
L E F T O V E R _ G R I T
L _ E _ N _ R _ N _ A _ O
J U M P I N G _ O X B O W
O _ U _ C _ E _ O _ O _ E
Y A R D _ T R A N Q U I L
```

15

```
_ S T U M P _ T E M P T _
G _ O _ A _ S _ J _ I _ F
R O W A N _ P R E T Z E L
U _ P _ G _ U _ C _ Z _ U
F L A V O U R _ T R A C K
F _ T _ _ N _ E _ _ _ _ E
_ S H O V E _ A D M I T _
S _ _ I _ E _ _ N _ _ T _
P A N I C _ Q U I C K L Y
I _ Y _ I _ U _ N _ L _ P
T O M B O L A _ E X I L E
E _ P _ U _ L _ P _ N _ D
_ C H A S M _ S T A G E _
```

16

```
I N J U R Y _ M E R G E D
N _ U _ A _ _ P _ N _ R _
F U N _ V E S T I B U L E
O _ C _ E _ U _ T _ _ _ S
R U T S _ S P L A S H E S
M _ I _ U _ E _ P _ A _ Y
_ O W N E R S H I P _ _ _
Q _ N _ E _ H _ S _ H _ A
U N S H A K E N _ M A I N
I _ _ R _ R _ U _ Z _ N _
F R A C T I O U S _ A X E
F _ R _ H _ _ E _ R _ X _
S A M O S A _ D R E D G E
```

17

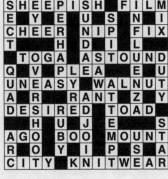

```
S H E E P I S H   F I L M
E   Y   E   U   S   N   I
C H E E R   N I P   F I X
T   H   D   I   L   
  T O G A   A S T O U N D
Q   V   P L E A   E   U
U N E A S Y   W A L N U T
A   R   R A N T   Z   Y
D E S I R E D   T O A D
    H   U   J   E     S
A G O   B O O   M O U N T
R   O   Y   I   P   S   A
C I T Y   K N I T W E A R
```

18

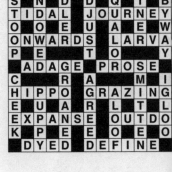

```
  R E T I N A   S I D E
S   N   D   D   Q   I   B
T I D A L   J O U R N E Y
O   O   E   U   A   E   W
O N W A R D S   L A R V A
P   E       T   O       Y
  A D A G E   P R O S E
C   R   A     M   I
H I P P O   G R A Z I N G
E   U   A   R   L   T   L
E X P A N S E   O U T D O
K   P   E   E   O   E   O
  D Y E D   D E F I N E
```

19

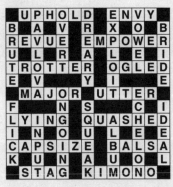

```
  U P H O L D   E N V Y
B   A   V   R   X   O   B
R E V U E   E M P O W E R
U   L   R   A   L   E   I
T R O T T E R   O G L E D
E   V       Y   I       E
  M A J O R   U T T E R
F       N   S     C   I
L Y I N G   Q U A S H E D
I   N   O   U   L   E   E
C A P S I Z E   B A L S A
K   U   N   A   U   O   L
  S T A G   K I M O N O
```

20

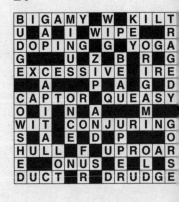

```
B I G A M Y   W   K I L T
U   A   I   W I P E   R
D O P I N G   G   Y O G A
G   U   Z   B   R   G
E X C E S S I V E   I R E
    A   P   A   G   D
C A P T O R   Q U E A S Y
O   I   N   A   M
W I T   C O N J U R I N G
S   A   E   D   P       O
H U L L   F   U P R O A R
E   O N U S   E   L   S
D U C T   R   D R U D G E
```

372

21

```
C U R S O R Y   U M B E R
O   E   U   A   N   R   U
P I L O T   W H I N I N G
I   I   G   N   T   G   B
O C C U R R E D   Z A N Y
U       O   D   P   N
S Q U A W K   S L U D G E
  P   N   E   E       T
F A W N   E X C A V A T E
E   A   J   O   S   R   R
V E R D I C T   A D O R N
E   D   L   I   N   M   A
R E S E T   C A T C A L L
```

22

```
S T A R V E   Q U A K E D
U   N   A   R   N   N   O
P A N A C H E   F J O R D
E   O   A   L   I   W   G
R A Y O N   A S T R I D E
B   C   X       N   D
  V I N Y L   U S A G E
O   N   S   E       I
V I V I D L Y   I D I O M
E   O   I   R   Z   N   P
R U L E R   U K U L E L E
D   V   G   P   R   R   D
O P E N E R   B E E T L E
```

23

```
F   S O P   I   T   T
E X P L O S I O N   R A W
E   A   Z   C   C   E   I
B E R S E R K   H U M U S
L       L       B   T
E L F   F L E X I B L E
R   O   A   C   E   L
  C O R D U R O Y   D Y E
J   T   E           N
A B H O R   S E R V I N G
U   O   I   C   O   R   T
N I L   S Q U E A M I S H
T   D   K   E   M   S   Y
```

24

```
H I J A C K   A B L A Z E
Y   U   H   O   P   I
B A D   A L I G N M E N T
R   I   R   N   E   H
I T C H   S T A M P E D E
D   I   S   R   E   X   R
  O S T E O P A T H
L   U   A   V   L   A   S
A S S O R T E D   Q U I P
W   K   R   S   S   H
F I N G E R T I P   T O E
U   I   R   U   E   R
L A T E S T   F R I D G E
```

Lexica
Solutions

Polygon
Solutions

Quintagram®
Solutions

Word Watch
Solutions

Codeword
Solutions

25

26

27

28

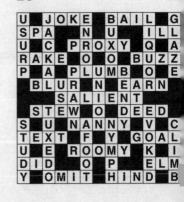

29

S	Q	U	E	A	K		C	O	B	W	E	B
	U		N		A		A		L		N	
P	E	R	J	U	R	E	D		A	X	L	E
	S		O		A		E		Z		I	
S	T	A	Y		O	U	T	W	E	I	G	H
	I		E		K						H	
F	O	N	D	U	E		R	E	M	O	T	E
	N				E		A		E			
S	N	O	W	D	R	O	P		G	O	N	G
	A		H		E		U		E		M	
K	I	W	I		A	T	T	E	N	D	E	E
	R		S		D		E		T		N	
V	E	S	T	R	Y		D	E	A	R	T	H

30

S	T	A	L	W	A	R	T		A	C	R	E
	Q		C		I		E		O		O	X
U	N	C	U	T		G	U	M	D	R	O	P
	I		U		H		A		N	G		E
D	I	S	H		F	R	U	I	T	I	O	N
	E			M		D		B		S		
T	I	D	I	E	D		J	U	M	B	L	E
W			R		B		S		O			
I	N	F	A	M	O	U	S		O	N	U	S
T		L		A		R		F	A		I	
C	R	E	V	I	C	E		A	N	N	E	X
H		C		D		A		W		Z		T
Y	O	K	E		Q	U	A	N	D	A	R	Y

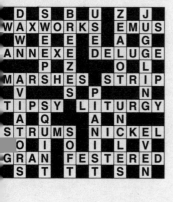

31

	D		S		B		U		Z		J	
W	A	X	W	O	R	K	S		E	M	U	S
	W		E		E		E		A		G	
A	N	N	E	X	E		D	E	L	U	G	E
			P		Z				O		L	
M	A	R	S	H	E	S		S	T	R	I	P
	V				S		P				N	
T	I	P	S	Y		L	I	T	U	R	G	Y
	A		Q				A		N			
S	T	R	U	M	S		N	I	C	K	E	L
	O		I		O		I		L		V	
G	R	A	N		F	E	S	T	E	R	E	D
	S		T		T		T		S		N	

32

	S	M	A	C	K		T	W	E	E	D	
J		A		O		T		E		N		C
U	R	N		S	Q	U	A	D		S	E	A
S		O				T				U		R
T	U	R	F		S	U	N		P	E	A	T
I			I	N	N		E	M	U			W
F	U	Z	Z		I		W		R	U	S	H
I		Z	I	P		E	G	G				E
A	W	A	Y		E	A	R		E	L	S	E
B		P				U				I		L
L	I	P		T	H	R	O	W		V	I	E
Y		L		O		A		A		I		D
	N	Y	L	O	N		E	X	U	D	E	

33

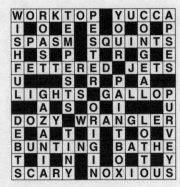

W	O	R	K	T	O	P		Y	U	C	C	A
I		O		E		O		O		O		P
S	P	A	S	M		S	Q	U	I	N	T	S
H		S		P		T		R		G		E
F	E	T	T	E	R	E	D		J	E	T	S
U				S		R		P		A		
L	I	G	H	T	S		G	A	L	L	O	P
		A		S		O		I				U
D	O	Z	Y		W	R	A	N	G	L	E	R
E		A		T		I		T		O		V
B	U	N	T	I	N	G		B	A	T	H	E
T		I		N		I		O		T		Y
S	C	A	R	Y		N	O	X	I	O	U	S

34

	Q	U	I	E	T	L	Y		L	A	I	R
A		V		X		E		U		M		A
S	C	U	T	T	L	E		B	R	A	S	S
H		L		R		W		I		Z		P
T	I	A	R	A		A	C	Q	U	I	T	
R				V		V		U		N		R
A	F	F	R	A	Y		J	I	G	G	L	E
Y		A		G		R		T				D
	S	T	R	A	F	E		O	C	C	U	R
T		A		N		B		U		O		A
R	E	L	I	C		U	N	S	C	R	E	W
I		L		E		K		L		A		
O	N	Y	X		R	E	C	Y	C	L	E	

35

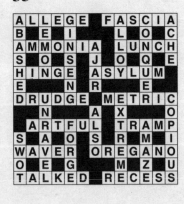

A	L	L	E	G	E		F	A	S	C	I	A
B		E		I		L		O		C		C
A	M	M	O	N	I	A		L	U	N	C	H
S		O		S		J		O		Q		E
H	I	N	G	E		A	S	Y	L	U	M	
E				N		R				E		
D	R	U	D	G	E		M	E	T	R	I	C
		N		A		X				O	
	A	R	T	F	U	L		T	R	A	M	P
S		A		O		S		R		M		I
W	A	V	E	R		O	R	E	G	A	N	O
O		E		G		M		Z		U	
T	A	L	K	E	D		R	E	C	E	S	S

36

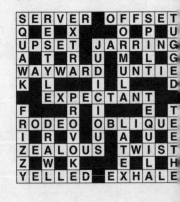

S	E	R	V	E	R		O	F	F	S	E	T
Q		E		X		O		P		U		U
U	P	S	E	T		J	A	R	R	I	N	G
A		T		R		U		M		L		G
W	A	Y	W	A	R	D		U	N	T	I	E
K		L		I		L		I		L		D
	E	X	P	E	C	T	A	N	T		
F		R		I		I		E		T
R	O	D	E	O		O	B	L	I	Q	U	E
I		R		V		U		A		U		E
Z	E	A	L	O	U	S		T	W	I	S	T
Z		W		K		E		L		H
Y	E	L	L	E	D		E	X	H	A	L	E

Lexica
Solutions

Polygon
Solutions

Quintagram®
Solutions

Word Watch
Solutions

Codeword
Solutions

37

```
M O I S T   R E P E L   O
  F   E V E   E   A G O
O F T E N   J U R O R   Z
P   R   E   P   V   E
E Q U I V O C A L   A D D
R   C   A   T   E   I
A L K A L I   E X E M P T
O   I   U   E   O   U
A P T   D A R E D E V I L
M   O   A   C   I   L
B   W I T C H   T H E R E
L E E   E   I C E   U
E   L A D E N   A G O N Y
```

38

```
I N I Q U I T Y   C R O P
N   N   S   H   A   U   I
L I E G E   E N D E M I C
A   X   S   I   J   B   K
Y E A R   B R O U H A H A
    C   B   S   S     X
G U T T E R   S T A P L E
U       E   R   S   R
F O O T S L O G   Y E L P
F   Z   W   C   S   T   U
A V O C A D O   U N Z I P
W   N   X   C   R   E   P
S E E R   J O Y F U L L Y
```

39

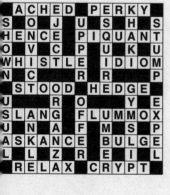

```
  A C H E D   P E R K Y
S   O   J   U   S   H   S
H E N C E   P I Q U A N T
O   V   C   P   U   K   U
W H I S T L E   I D I O M
N   C   R       R       P
  S T O O D   H E D G E
U   R   O       Y   E
S L A N G   F L U M M O X
U   N   A   F   M   S   P
A S K A N C E   B U L G E
L   L   Z   R   E   I   L
  R E L A X   C R Y P T
```

40

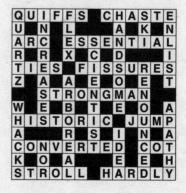

```
Q U I F F S   C H A S T E
U   N   L   A   K   N
A R C   E S S E N T I A L
R   R   X   C   D       I
T I E S   F I S S U R E S
Z   A   A E   O   E   T
    S T R O N G M A N
W   E   B   T   E   O   A
H I S T O R I C   J U M P
A   R   S   I   N   A
C O N V E R T E D   C O T
K   O   A       E   E   H
S T R O L L   H A R D L Y
```

Lexica
Solutions

Polygon
Solutions

Quintagram®
Solutions

Word Watch
Solutions

Codeword
Solutions

41

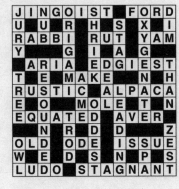

```
J I N G O I S T   F O R D
U   U   R   H S   X I   I
R A B B I   R U T   Y A M
Y     G   I   A G
  A R I A   E D G I E S T
T E   M A K E   N   H
R U S T I C   A L P A C A
E   O   M O L E   T   N
E Q U A T E D   A V E R
    N   R   D   D     Z
O L D   O D E   I S S U E
W   E   D   S   N   P   S
L U D O   S T A G N A N T
```

42

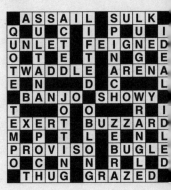

```
  A S S A I L   S U L K
Q   U C   I   P   U   I
U N L E T   F E I G N E D
O   T   E   T   N   G   E
T W A D D L E   A R E N A
E   N     D   C       L
  B A N J O   S H O W Y
T     O   O     R     I
E X E R T   B U Z Z A R D
M   P   T   L   E   N   L
P R O V I S O   B U G L E
O   C   N   N   R   L   D
  T H U G   G R A Z E D
```

43

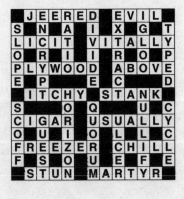

```
  J E E R E D   E V I L
S   N   A   I   X   G   T
L I C I T   V I T A L L Y
O   R   I   I   R   O   P
P L Y W O O D   A B O V E
E   P       E   C     D
  I T C H Y   S T A N K
S     O   Q     U   C
C I G A R   U S U A L L Y
O   U   I   O   L   L   C
F R E E Z E R   C H I L L
F   S   O   U   E   F   E
  S T U N   M A R T Y R
```

44

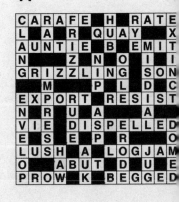

```
C A R A F E   H   R A T E
L   A   R   Q U A Y     X
A U N T I E   B   E M I T
N     Z   N   O   I   I
G R I Z Z L I N G   S O N
    M     P   L D   C
E X P O R T   R E S I S T
N   R   U   A     A
V I E   D I S P E L L E D
E   S   E   P   R     O
L U S H   A   L O G J A M
O     A B U T   D   U   E
P R O W   K   B E G G E D
```

45

```
S E C L U D E   M A D A M
W   L   N   X   I   I   I
E V E N T   P O M P O U S
E   A   O   E   E   C   E
T H R O W I N G   J E E R
L       A   D   V   S
Y O G U R T   F I N E S T
    L   D   O   R       H
B O O K   O B S T A C L E
A   B   M   E   U   O   A
S Q U E A K Y   O R B I T
I   L   Z   E   U   R   R
S W E D E   D E S C A L E
```

46

```
U N P I C K   S T R I N G
N   L   A   F   O   M   A
J O U R N A L   P E A R L
U   M   V   U   A   G   O
S E P I A   F I Z Z I E R
T       S   F       N   E
  Q U A S H   S P I E D
P   P       B   O       M
A E R O S O L   S I D L E
Y   I   I   E   T   O   N
O R G A N   E L B O W E D
U   H   G   P   O   S   E
T E T H E R   E X T E N D
```

47

```
S   A   H   D   T   D   J
P E R S O N I F Y   E Y E
E   E   L   N   R   L   L
A B A N D O N   E Q U A L
K       E       S   Y
E G O   H O R R I F I C
R   U   O   V   O   B
  S T O W A W A Y   N I L
S   S   O       I
C O M M A   E L E M E N T
U   A   C   F   V   X   Z
F U R   H O U S E W I F E
F   T   E   L   R   T   D
```

48

```
B I T I N G   A B A C U S
L   E   E   E   O   A
A L L   W I T H S T O O D
Z   E   S   A   O       D
E N V Y   P R O T O C O L
R   I   B   A   T   U   E
  S T E R N N E S S
J   E   A   T   D   T   Q
U N D E R C U T   T O F U
I   S   L   T   M   A
C H E C K M A T E   A R K
E   N   I       X   R   E
R I D I N G   S T A Y E D
```

Lexica
Solutions

Polygon
Solutions

Quintagram®
Solutions

Word Watch
Solutions

Codeword
Solutions

49

S	K	E	W	E	R		V	E	T	T	E	D
	N		R		E		O		I		A	
S	I	L	E	N	C	E	D		M	A	R	K
	F		A		O		K		E		R	
Z	E	S	T		U	N	A	F	R	A	I	D
	H		N				N				N	
	Q	U	E	S	T	I	O	N	I	N	G	
	U				R		N					
R	E	J	O	I	C	E	D		E	N	V	Y
	L		U		O		E		X		A	
P	L	O	T		V	E	R	B	A	L	L	Y
	E		D		E		E		C		U	
A	D	J	O	I	N		D	O	T	T	E	D

50

	C		H		P		F		C		R	
J	O	Y	O	U	S		A	V	O	W	E	D
	N		L		Y		S		H		V	
S	T	U	D		C	O	C	K	E	R	E	L
	E				H		I		R		L	
E	X	A	S	P	E	R	A	T	E	D		
	T		H					N		S		
		R	E	Q	U	I	S	I	T	I	O	N
	O		A		N		T				U	
O	V	E	R	T	U	R	E		S	I	L	L
	A		I		S		A		I		F	
B	R	O	N	Z	E		M	A	G	N	U	M
	Y		G		D		Y		H		L	

51

F	L	O	S	S		P	A	R	T	A	K	E
O		C		W		A		E		X		N
R	E	T	R	I	A	L		C	H	E	S	T
M		A		L		E						I
A	N	G	U	L	A	R		I	N	G	O	T
L		O		E		P		R		R		Y
	I	N	Q	U	I	S	I	T	I	O	N	
S		A		N		I				V		F
P	O	L	K	A		T	R	A	P	E	Z	E
R				L				I		L		N
A	L	I	B	I		J	O	S	T	L	E	D
N		L		K		O		L		E		E
G	A	L	L	E	R	Y		E	R	R	E	D

52

A		G	R	U	B		S	O	Y	A		B
B	R	A		O		Q		N		I	L	
O		T		F	O	R	U	M		N		I
V	E	E	R		T		I		J	E	S	T
E		A		S	H	A	D	Y		X		Z
	H	U	S	H		L		I	D	E	A	
		L	E	A	T	H	E	R				
	S	T	Y	E		A		L	Y	N	X	
A		A		T	I	R	E	D		U		N
W	O	K	E		N		N		I	D	L	Y
F		I		A	C	U	T	E		I		M
U	R	N		U		E		S	O	P		H
L		G	E	A	R		R	O	O	M		H

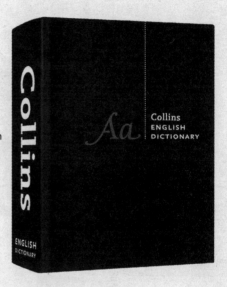

THE  TIMES

Shop the full range of Times Books from world-famous atlases and puzzle books to Amazing Places and great lives – there's something for everyone at timesbooks.co.uk.

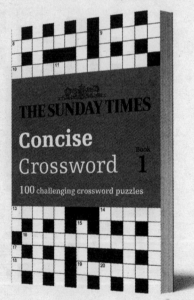